ABOUT SCOUT SCAR

*Looking into a
Cumbrian landscape*

Jan Wiltshire

First published in 2008
by Palatine Books,
Carnegie House,
Chatsworth Road
Lancaster LA1 4SL
www.palatinebooks.com

British Library Cataloguing-in-Publication data
A catalogue record for this book is available from the British Library

ISBN: 978-1-874181-57-6

Designed and typeset by Carnegie Book Production
www.carnegiebookproduction.com
Printed and bound in the UK by Alden Press

ABOUT SCOUT SCAR

Looking into a Cumbrian landscape

Jan Wiltshire

Foreword and acknowledgements

Out on an exploration, I go where the day suggests. The lure might be an influx of migrating birds, or rarities flowering or fruiting on an escarpment edge that call for a degree of venturesomeness if I'm to take a closer look, or a startling outcropping of fungi that shows once and never again. There is excitement in the unexpected and, on making a discovery, I go back again and again to observe and to note the shifting patterns of the seasons with all their quirks and irregularities. It is special to find wildlife for oneself and to begin to see into the ecology of a particular environment. The learning experience is infinite and that's part of the enjoyment too.

I've always loved to write and this book is in the tradition of Nature writing. I have the habit of writing journals: on the day and of the day. I like to feel at one with a landscape: to be so focused that nothing intrudes on what is taking place right there before my eyes. The aim is to distil the essence of an experience: to capture those inspirational moments in writing. Some excursions were recorded in letters to my friend David Hunt (who drew the three original maps) so occasional extracts feature alongside journals. This book took me unawares. I was well underway before I realised that was where I was heading. It evolved and grew. I had become more and more caught up with the birds, flora and fungi I was finding, and I was learning the way different habitats worked. I was making connections.

There was a key moment in spring 2006 when the journey took on a new direction, a new dimension. I began to look at this well-known landscape afresh and to ask why it looks as it does, who makes the countryside? The history of land ownership and management influences the appearance of a landscape and I began to delve, spurred on by conversations with local farmers Tony Chapman and Brian Bowness . Everyone in the farming community was eager to help, generous with information and with a keen interest in what I was about. Their voices and their intimate knowledge of the area are dispersed throughout the book and underpin it. I should like to thank them all, and the Hound Trailing community too.

Key locations, including Helsington Barrows and Brigsteer Park, are owned and managed by the National Trust at Sizergh, and Brian Fereday, Forester Warden, has been generous with the help he has given me. Natural England has an interest in Cunswick Scar and Scout Scar because they are Sites of Special Scientific Interest with European importance for wildlife. Conservation is under their aegis and they are working closely with farmers: an interaction that is vital and dynamic.

My thanks to David Silk for information regarding the refurbishment of the Mushroom Shelter. And to Howard Robinson regarding the toposcope by St John's Church. I should like to thank all those local people whom I have met during the course of writing the book, whose names appear within the text to indicate the help they have given. My thanks to friends who have been supportive throughout and have helped in diverse ways: exploring with me, reading my typescript and helping with IT and constructing maps. Any mistakes in this book, however, are entirely my own.

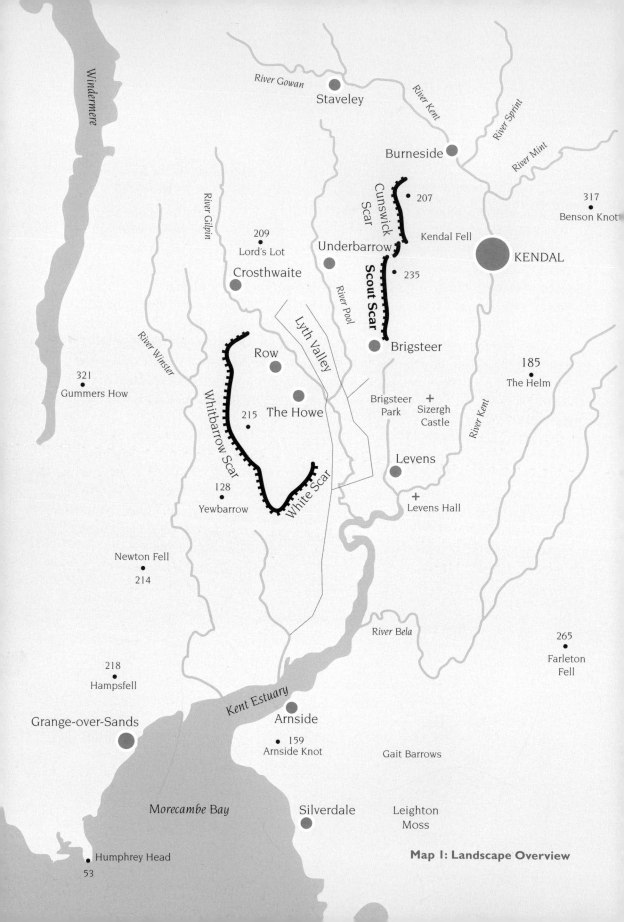

Windermere

River Gowan

Staveley

River Kent

River Sprint

Burneside

River Mint

River Gilpin

207

317
Benson Knott

Cunswick Scar

209
Lord's Lot

Underbarrow

Kendal Fell

Crosthwaite

235

KENDAL

River Pool

Scout Scar

River Winster

Lyth Valley

Brigsteer

Row

185
The Helm

321
Gummers How

Whitbarrow Scar

215

The Howe

Brigsteer Park

Sizergh Castle

River Kent

128
Yewbarrow

White Scar

Levens

Newton Fell

214

Levens Hall

River Bela

265
Farleton Fell

218
Hampsfell

Kent Estuary

Grange-over-Sands

Arnside

159
Arnside Knot

Gait Barrows

Morecambe Bay

Silverdale

Leighton Moss

Humphrey Head

53

Map 1: Landscape Overview

Landscape Overview

On its swift, short course to its estuary at Morecambe Bay the River Kent flows through the market town of Kendal, which is situated on the north-eastern edge of a belt of limestone hugging the volcanics of the central Lake District. The Kent estuary penetrates these Morecambe Bay limestones, the character name by which the area is known, and there is a diversity of limestone features including a series of escarpments; Hampsfell, Yewbarrow, Whitbarrow, Cunswick Scar and Scout Scar, the latter being about two kilometres west of Kendal. Each of these escarpments has a north to south alignment, with its scarp slope facing west, its dip slope to the east.

This area of carboniferous limestone was subject to the scouring of glaciation during the Ice Age. Limestone is permeable and fast draining, due to its network of open joints, so once the last of the ice had retreated and the permafrost had gone there was little further surface water erosion. The dry valleys which characterise the landscape would have been deepened during the period of glaciation. There is little standing water on these uplands and the aerial view shows outcropping bands of rock above the cliffs of the Whitbarrow scarp and extensive exposed limestone on the broad ridges of Whitbarrow and Scout Scar. This often occurs as frost-shattered rafts of clitter, most conveniently to hand for the building of the dry stone walls whose signature is the sharp edges of its pure white limestone and the grey and black lichens associated with this alkaline rock. The glaciers transported much debris, including weighty objects and, as the ice melted, deposited them onto the scoured limestone bedrock so that a boulder of alien rock sits on a limestone plinth, like a sculpture. These glacial erratics have bright lichens that indicate acid rock. Glaciers dumped their boulders but carried finer debris out to Morecambe Bay, and silts and sands were blown onto Whitbarrow and Scout Scar to form pockets of loess in dips and hollows of the limestone. In these acid soils heather grows and offers shelter and a micro-habitat.

At 235 metres Scout Scar is marginally higher than Whitbarrow (215m) and Hampsfell (218m) but each offers magnificent views of the surrounding countryside.

These ridges and escarpments are exposed to the prevailing south westerlies which, on Whitbarrow especially, create wind-blasted yew trees that resemble dark pennons. With no standing water, poor soils and lack of nutrients, scattered trees grow stunted amongst rafts of limestone clitter and there are native juniper, yew and hawthorn on the broad ridges.

Whitbarrow

Whitbarrow – the white hill – and to the south the dramatic cliff of White Scar. In sunlight, light bright Whitbarrow. There are a few clusters of larch and birch but it is an open ridge with blue moor grass, a spring and summer flush of limestone flora and a wealth of butterflies. Sections of the cliffs and screes of its scarp slope are concealed by hanging woods. On gloomy days, these limestone escarpments have a somewhat forbidding appearance with dark yew rooted in fissures in the rock face, and Black Yews Scar, below Lord's Seat, is an evocative name. East of the viewpoint of Lord's Seat, the dip slope is broken by a series of minor stepped limestone scarps with yew and juniper rooted into the rock and swept and sculpted into strange shapes. And above each shallow cliff there is a shelf of limestone pavement with clint and gryke formation. Hampsfell and Whitbarrow have open and wooded limestone pavement, a habitat which Scout Scar lacks. Hidden within the trees on Whitbarrow is Gillbirks Quarry which provided building stone for Kendal. Farms, and the famous damson orchards of the Lyth Valley, are situated low on the sheltered dip slope at the spring line where permeable limestone is downfaulted against impervious Silurian slates and greywackes. The hamlets of Row and the Howe are surrounded by an intake wall and fields whose old boundaries have all the quirks and irregularities of an English landscape.

The Lyth Valley

Between the limestone escarpments of Whitbarrow and Scout Scar lies the Lyth Valley. Its river, the Gilpin, has its confluence with the River Kent almost at its estuary as it debouches into Morecambe Bay. Looking down upon its broad flood plain from Scout Scar, it still resembles an inlet of the sea with White Scar, the cliff at the southern tip of Whitbarrow, a headland looking out over the bay. The topography suggests it and winter flooding highlights this impression as the eye scans across flooded pastures and out to sea.

When sunlight gleams on flood waters the pattern of the comparatively recent man-made landscape is emphasised and there is a geometric and angular look about the network of roads and fields, each bordered by hedge and drainage ditch. With deep ditches on either side, roads are often elevated and hump-back bridges span drain and river. From the height of Scout Scar the grassy embankments of Underbarrow Pool show clearly. Drainage in the Lyth Valley has layers historical and physical, with a higher system and a lower system that channels water underneath the river. A nexus of drains and ditches converges on the pumping stations on which agriculture in the valley depends. There is a handful of rocky knolls and outcrops dignified with the name of hill; Dobdale Hill is shown on the OS map at 10 metres, a single ring contour, whilst High Heads has a spot height of 24 metres. Farmsteads are situated just on the limestone where it meets the alluvial pasture and most farms include some of each type of land: hard land and moss. Cinderbarrow is at an elevation of 20 metres, just south of the wooded scarp slope of Brigsteer Park. Park End Farm is at 30 metres.

When these older farms were built the Lyth Valley was an area of wetland, a raised bog drained only by the ditches of the peat workings. The River Gilpin was tidal and reached as far as Underbarrow, depositing sand with each tide. The essential wetland nature of the Lyth Valley is declared on the OS map by the numerous *mosses, drains, dikes* and *ditches.* These peat mosses were a source of fuel for Kendal but by the end of the 19th century the town was no longer dependent on the peat which was gradually being worked out. Park Moss, on the flood plain below Brigsteer Park, was well placed to supply Sizergh Castle with fuel. Peat was stored in peat cotes and Cotes is shown on the OS map just below the limestone scar bank at Levens, where peat cutters lived. At Row, on the western side of the valley, there is a peat house built mid-18th century as a peat store for the farm and now a holiday cottage.

The appearance of the Lyth Valley landscape was transformed early in the 19th century with the reclamation of the mosses subsequent to the Heversham Enclosure Act and Award. A comprehensive drainage system was introduced and the main drain through the centre of the valley dates from that time. Catchwaters were dug to divert spring water from the slopes of the valley: the western catchwater is a drain to collect run-off from the dip slope of Whitbarrow and pump it out to the sea. The eastern catchwater runs below Brigsteer Park, where the wooded limestone scarp slope meets peat at Park Moss, continuing past Cotes and Levens to empty directly into the River Kent. The mosses were drained, birch trees began to colonise, and across the Lyth Valley there are pockets of birch and oak woodland. Wetland habitat was lost and with the acidic peat removed there was a black, alluvial soil with blue clay close beneath. To prepare the land for arable farming, quantities of lime were spread and there are numerous lime kilns, like the cluster about Row low down on the Whitbarrow dip slope, where limestone was readily available to process for use as a fertiliser during the reclamation of the mosses. The pattern of Lyth Valley fields and their encompassing ditches dates from that time, the geometric design made possible by the flood plain. Near Cotes, off Quagg's Road, there is a cluster of narrow field strips which were rights of common of turbary where a household worked its peat. Roads were laid over the mosses and, like the sequence of Moss Lanes in the vicinity of Tullythwaite Hall, they attempt to provide access to all the fields.

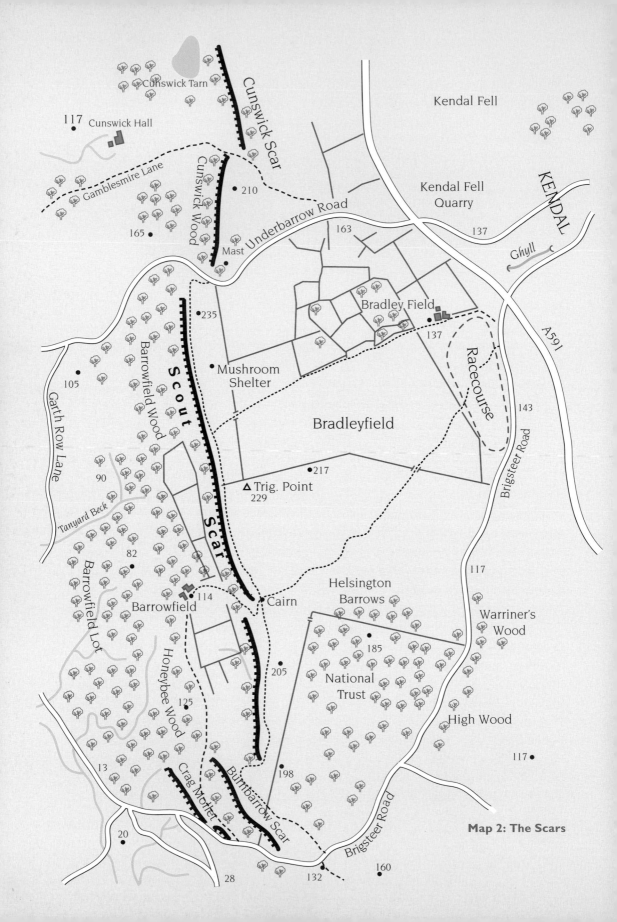

Map 2: The Scars

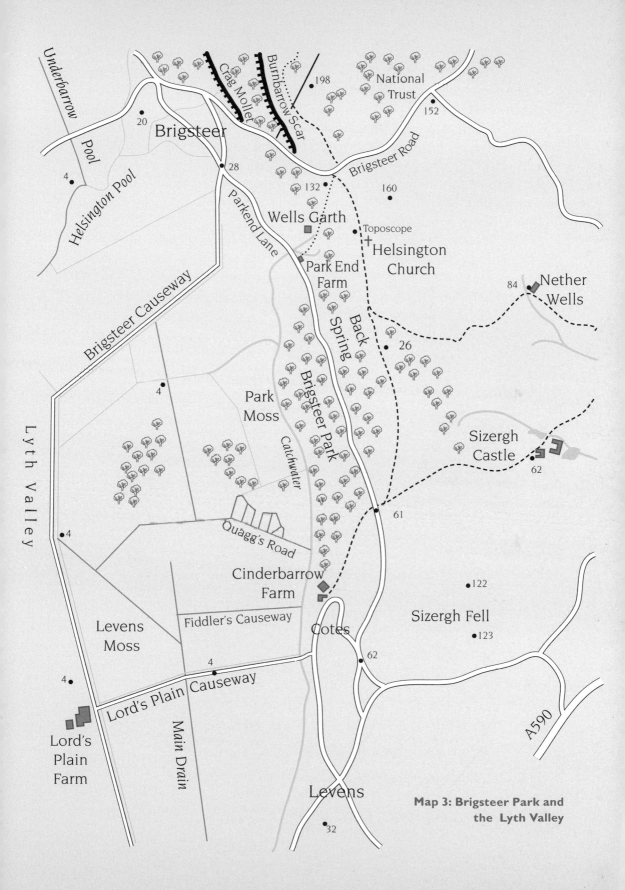

Map 3: Brigsteer Park and
the Lyth Valley

Today, there is little arable farming in the valley. At Lord's Plain, a significantly low-lying farm built shortly after enclosure and the reclamation of the mosses, they graze sheep and rear black and white Holstein Friesian cattle. The farm is a tenancy of the Levens Hall estate. At Cinderbarrow Farm, they have a dairy herd of Jerseys and a thousand sheep. Over four kilometres to the north, at Tullythwaite Hall, they have Holstein Friesian dairy cattle. All these farmers make silage for their cattle. The farmers spread a ground and powdered limestone as a spring fertiliser but this is only applied once in ten or fifteen years. Ground limestone comes from a local quarry at Silverdale.

The pumping system copes, apart from exceptional rains when there is flooding, but the water doesn't rise fast so there is no drowning, though when it is very wet sheep may have to be moved to fields less prone to flooding. With the construction of the A590 dual carriageway, doors were fixed beneath it at Sampool Bridge so the River Gilpin is no longer tidal and this makes maintenance of drains and ditches somewhat easier. The maintenance regime accords with National Environmental Agency directives: farmers must not plough or cultivate right up to the hedges and fertiliser must not be introduced into the ditches. At Lord's Plain Farm they have 3 ½ miles of ditches to maintain and a contractor flails the hedges and mows out the ditches to give the water a free run. They are dredged every five years to clean mud out at the bottom.

The protection and restoration of wetland habitat, of aquatic habitat, in Cumbria and in the Lyth Valley is encouraged by conservation bodies and there are already nature reserves at Foulshaw Moss, which is a raised peat bog on the Kent estuary.

Glossary

Aurora Borealis: the Northern Lights. Boreal indicates northern.

Breccia: composite rock with angular fragments of stone.

Bund: an artificial embankment to keep in(or to hold back) water.

Cheval de frise: an iron-tipped barrier of stakes intended to deter a cavalry charge- here a barrier of low, spiny branches difficult to penetrate.

Clint: rock projecting between cracks. A limestone feature.

Clitter: a mass of shattered stones. Frost-shattered limestone.

Grike or gryke: a crack or fissure in carboniferous limestone.

Mille feuille: limestone resembling compressed layers of leaves.

On the qui vive: alert, on the look-out, wide-awake.

Pyroclastic rock: originating in the vast heat of a volcano.

Scout: indicates crag or cliff. eg Jack Scout, Kinder Scout.

Scar: a cliff, crag or precipice. Scout and Scar echo around the same notion.

Spicula: a fine splinter or fragment.

Taiga: temperate coniferous forest, as found in Finland and Norway.

The Scars (Map 2)

This escarpment of carboniferous limestone is a dramatic landscape feature and defines habitat. Cunswick Scar, Scout Scar and Burnbarrow Scar have cliffs, scree buttresses and steeply wooded slopes. Barrowfield Farm is below the escarpment and its sheltered pastures are surrounded by woodland. The exposed ridge rises to 235 metres. Bradleyfield Farm is on the escarpment dip slope and its in-bye land offers shelter, with dry stone walls and fringes of mature trees about its pastures. The walled National Trust area of Helsington Barrows is parkland habitat, unlike the zone immediately to its north.

Brigsteer Park and the Lyth Valley (Map 3)

Here farming and conservation are under the aegis of the National Trust at Sizergh. Park End and Cinderbarrow are National Trust farms and the Trust owns and manages Helsington Barrows and Brigsteer Park. The escarpment of carboniferous limestone runs south through Brigsteer Park toward Levens and the Kent estuary. The catchwater marks the foot of the scarp slope and to the west lie the mosses of the Lyth Valley.

1999

29 September 1999: on Scout Scar

To introduce visitors to Scout Scar, to show off my new place, there needed to be good visibility. If there was much cloud cover they had to imagine the panorama. We set off for an afternoon walk in the rain and all the way to the escarpment the light grew stronger and the views more dramatic. Dark rain clouds encircled us but blue sky opened up directly above. A rainbow arced over Kendal and the Yorkshire Dales to the east and the slender ash trees on the limestone clitter gleamed ethereal and sunlit against an intense and darkening mass of cloud. Our voices echoed from beneath the domed roof of the Mushroom Shelter and we marvelled at the bright-rimmed clouds, the interplay of light and darkness all about us and our good fortune in being at the sunlit centre of dramatic weather.

Next day, we went back. Mist hung below in the Lyth Valley and we could just make out the Kent estuary in the direction of Morecambe Bay. A flock of sheep came running toward us and we heard the whistle of the farmer to his dog. There were four men gathering sheep to take them down to Barrowfield Farm for dipping and to introduce the tups to the ewes. They need the better grazing of the pastures about Barrowfield, the in-bye land, to be in prime condition before mating. There the ewes are given feed during the winter when they are in lamb. Swaledale ewes and lambs have had spring and summer grazing up here for the last twelve years. It's a distinctive breed, with round horns, a black face with a white muzzle and black or speckled legs. In the farmer's opinion this is one of the best views in the Lake District, and a toposcope at the Mushroom Shelter pinpoints the encircling fells so walkers may identify them.

5 October 1999: Scout Scar

Dawn at this time of year can be captivating. High on its moraine, Kendal Castle and its trees broke clear of the mist that hung over the River Kent: mist that swelled and diffused, now opaque, now translucent and shot through with sunlight which showed up two plumes of smoke as a denser whiteness within the vapour. And the warm colours preceding the sunrise made the sky glorious. An arc of rainbow hung vivid over the town and the breath of a few folk out and about was visible in the chilly morning air.

A few withered spikes of autumn gentian remained and heather was seeding in brownish hue. It takes a day of outstanding clarity, of strong sunlight and shadow, to see the architecture of the fells and this was just such a morning, cold and clear.

For a few moments Kentmere and Ill Bell were illuminated, Pike o' Stickle showed out of the darkness with a band of light upon it. The drama in the skyscape was breathtaking as the sun vied with cloud and triumphed.

17 October 1999: *Scout Scar*

Not a day for vistas, there was bright sun but no clarity so I focused on what was close at hand. I walked north above the escarpment with the sun shining a spotlight into the wood below. Fieldfare were calling and their pale underwings caught the light in a grove of dark yew rooted in the limestone scree of the buttress directly below the cliff edge. Scores of fieldfare fed on yew berries whose fleshy red arils glowed in the sombre foliage. Above the now steeper escarpment, I found a vantage point where I was half hidden in heather and could watch them foraging beneath the yew and flying above the canopy. Seclusion: the life of the wood had hold of me.

Scout Scar escarpment. The scarp slope shows cliff terrace, grassy buttress, a grove of native yew trees in scree with a strip of mixed wood below. The green pasture of Barrowfield Farm contrasts with the rough grazing on the high ridge to the right of the image. 27.3.2008

The wood follows the line of the escarpment and sometimes spreads wide, so that it affords shelter and the perfect feeding ground for mistlethrush, redwing and fieldfare. It's a thrushfest as the yew arils ripen. The limestone escarpment runs from Cunswick Scar, curving south through Scout Scar, Burnbarrow Scar and Crag Mollet to Brigsteer Park. In places, the cliff is precipitous and sheer. There are stretches where steep buttresses abut shallow cliff terraces, and there are shelving slopes of grass and limestone scree where the scarp slope is broken up and gentler. Native yew trees and whitebeam favour the steep, upper fringe of buttresses and sometimes grow in the cliff face. Often, the escarpment is obscured by trees and to see it one needs to look up toward it from Barrowfield Farm. To see it entire it is best to be significantly west. On the ridge above the cliff it's a different habitat: an exposed and open landscape of limestone scrub.

20 October 1999: *Scout Scar*

Once more there was strong sunlight to create magical effects over woods and escarpment, with merely a hint of the Coniston fells and the Langdales. My woods are wonderful, with deciduous trees burnished in metallic hues and the stunted ash trees high on the exposed scarp slope already stripped of leaves. Always a light, bright wood because of the limestone and the scattering of slender ash trees. The wind stirs each kind of tree to a distinctive note for Thomas Hardy, who listens to arboreal voices as he begins *Under The Greenwood Tree.* Today, the wind roared like the sea to drown out most of the fieldfare calls. Below me, they flew dark above the canopy and came fluttering silver to feed in evergreen yew. There are glossy-leaved holly and pines seemingly growing on the cliff face. Fieldfare are not confiding birds and when I found a shelf to sit and watch with my back to the cliff they spied me and soon the trees were silent again. I am making the place mine by taking pleasure in the changes of the season and by venturing here, not least in bracing weather, to find a vantage point on the crag face.

6 November 1999: *Scout Scar and the Mushroom Shelter*

The first sprinkling of snow on the high fells. A north-west wind and you could see for miles. Met a local walking the path above the escarpment who told me the home guard used to meet on Scout Scar at the Mushroom Shelter, as the rotunda is known locally. Within its dome the locations of the fells are inscribed, so you may stand at the axis of the cross-shaped shelter and align yourself to name all that you can see.

23 November 1999: *at home*

There had been an extended spell of glorious weather: cold, clear and bright. It concluded on the day Margaret arrived from Bristol and warmer, wetter weather took hold. My birding mentor since I joined Bristol Ornithological Club in 1984, she duly arrived with telescope and as she was carrying it indoors I told her that a waxwing had recently been sighted in the neighbourhood, so I was eager to go looking. 'Have you berries?' she asked. I moved to a kitchen window to point out a hybrid rowan which had been a mass of golden leaves and red berries. Something was sitting huddled in its bare, fruitless branches but I was wearing reading glasses so dismissed it as 'just a lump of stuff'. No need to look further, there it was. She ran to root out her binoculars, mine were right there in the kitchen. It was about 2.00 pm so we had the best light of a dull day and the waxwing was so close. The coincidence of it amused us both.

Kendal Racecourse with Bradleyfield Farm ewes about to lamb. Easter Sunday 23.3.2008

2000

19 January 2000: Beast Banks

I walked through the ghyll track where tussocks of grass were stiff with frost and sounds of dripping came from trees as the power of the sun took effect. On the Brigsteer Road pavement there seemed to be fragments of glass from an accident but under the next overhanging tree, and the next, the same. Was it glass? A child cried out and the mother comforted her children and told them with wonder in her voice that ice was showering down from the trees. From the beeches of Beast Banks fell tiny frozen lozenges. The ground steamed as the morning sun met last night's ice and houses billowed out their central heating gases. A fieldfare, brilliant of plumage, feasted on a berried shrub and the evergreen conifers were full of fluttering wings.

Today, Beast Banks is a grassy space with grand beech trees. On John Todd's map of 1787 it is shown as Beast Banks or Beast Fair and it was an open air cattle market with open air slaughterhouse set up there. Postman Pat's Post Office, recently closed, is located there.

1 March 2000: St David's Day on Scout Scar
(from letter to David)

I heard lark ascending and watched a buzzard soar on a thermal that carried it along Scout Scar escarpment whilst a flapping rook tried to see it off. Fresh snow on the tops. Great visibility with sunlight and shadow to reveal the architecture of a sweep of distant fells. Since Saturday, I've been studying the maps and from the Mushroom Shelter I looked directly at our last week's route to Wetherlam Edge and Pike o' Blisco and Bowfell. I was lucky to see it on a day of such clarity. A beautiful morning and a coda to our grand winter walk.

16 March 2000: Wells Garth and Brigsteer Park

From St John's Church we followed a footpath down the wooded scarp slope to Wells Garth: a water garden as its name declares, with comfrey, scillas and tête à tête daffodils. Water issues from the limestone, cascades over rock, trickles down the path and into the waterfalls that flow down to Park End Farm, down into the catchwater that takes this spring water off the fell, and out into the Kent estuary and Morecambe Bay. How delightful the sound of a beck in this limestone landscape! And there is water mint and *Veronica becabunga*. An idyllic spot.

Wild daffodils and hazel coppice.

Brigsteer Park is semi-natural woodland, with coppicing. There are some mature trees, good habitat for birds, from the 1960s planting: western hemlock and western red cedar. Once part of the Sizergh Estate, the wood is now managed by the National Trust. It lies on the escarpment scarp slope but there are pockets of clay and of sand plastered on the limestone which shelves under peat just before it meets the catchwater, and to the west lie Park Moss and the Lyth Valley: agricultural land with different geology and habitat.

Swathes of delicate, wild daffodils bloomed amongst the coppiced hazel, their petals paler than their trumpets and facing the sun. In the upper wood we found an uprooted tree with blooms flourishing in the earth-covered roots. There were daffodils amongst the winter leaf litter, amongst the heaps of brashings and the brambles in which small birds like to nest. Like many of the flowers of the field layer, they need good light levels if they are to bloom. The constantly changing heights of growing shrubs and trees would block out light and, without careful management, only daffodil leaves would show. The dynamics of woodland growth ensure that every year will be different and these plants take advantage to grow and flower in maximum light before the leaf canopy appears. Creating space for more growth gives everything a chance. Native ash, which is associated with limestone, casts a light shade with the open shape of the tree and its serrated leaflets. Beech has been thinned out because it isn't native here, its leaf litter acidifies the soil and its heavier shade inhibits the flowering of bluebells. Brigsteer Park is primarily broadleaf woodland with ash, birch, oak and small-leaved lime, and an understorey of hazel, hawthorn, blackthorn and guelder rose.

Wandering the woodland paths, our attention drifted from daffodils to a view through the coppice of the Coniston fells and the Langdales.

31 March 2000: Ullswater, Watermillock and Troutbeck Church

Yesterday my friend Fiona introduced me to Brigsteer Park and now we were
on a pilgrimage to the shore of Ullswater. In April 1802, Dorothy Wordsworth
recorded in her journal the find of wild daffodils that William later drew upon.
She has a freshness and a spontaneity not to be found in her brother's poem,
in the view of the poet U.A. Fanthorpe.

Troutbeck Churchyard was aglow with a fine display of not-altogether-wild
daffodils.

28 August 2000: Scout Scar

Autumn gentian were abundant in the short grass but hard to spot unless the
sun opened the flowers. Louring clouds today, and fine rain over the Lyth Valley.
A most unusual rainbow, seen close to the ground and draped arcless toward
the north east. Everyone has a personal rainbow with sun, oneself and prism in
unique relation. Particular to oneself. That's true of vision. Impossible to envisage
what someone else is seeing: a question both of imagination and of visual acuity.

2000: the toposcope by St John's Church, Helsington

At 125 metres, St John's Church has a fine, elevated position. A pasture, often
grazed by sheep and sometimes cattle, slopes down to a woodland fringe which
conceals the crags where limestone meets impermeable rock and springs burst
forth at Wells Garth. In 2000 a millenium toposcope was erected, looking out
across the Lyth Valley: to the north the Langdale Pikes and sweeping south the
Coniston fells, Whitbarrow, Humphrey Head, Morecambe Bay and landscapes
of the Kent estuary. It was designed by Howard Robinson of Brigsteer, who
sketched and photographed fells prior to mapping them. He laid a concrete base
strengthened with steel bars, and his brother Duncan assembled the tripartite
dry stone structure using donated Levens flat stone, a local limestone. His outline
map is presented on three stainless steel insets: a triptych encased in stone. The
structure resembles the slabs of a stone altar. At Eastertide, the pasture filled with
ewes and their lambs who queued to approach the altar and to squeeze back and
forth between the slabs, rubbing to ease an itch, easing an itch and dislodging a
stone or two. This lack of reverence led to the pointing of the dry stone structure
and now all is well.

2001

Concerning the Foot and Mouth epidemic

Things go awry. My broken wrist was healed after an accident in the New Zealand rain forest and I drove home from Bristol eager for some fell walking. From the M6, I saw fires on the hillside at Burton-in-Kendal, fires to consume the carcases of infected animals; an early case of Foot and Mouth in what was to be the worst epidemic since 1967. It began, allegedly, at Heddon Wall, a farm in Northumberland on Hadrian's Wall.

There was a week of glorious winter weather as the epidemic spread and government measures came into force to restrict movement of stock and public footpaths were closed. Sunday 4th March, and I was already yearning to be out there on the sunlit, snow-sprinkled fells. Access to the countryside looked set to be prohibited for months and months to come. Every gatepost, every stile, was festooned with red and white no-entry tape with notices barring access in accordance with the Foot and Mouth Act: official, clearly printed government vetos with a £5,000 fine for transgressors. On the track which leads to Bradleyfield Farm there was a pile of disinfected straw and the rooks made for it, flying off with straws for nesting material – a disinfected rookery. Movement of stock was prohibited. A farmer said ruefully that his wife had left him and now he couldn't even talk to his sheep. It was spring, lambing time, with all those newborn animals being put down! Farmers struggled not to break down as they were interviewed. 'Don't watch them die', one warned.

With Scout Scar and the fells off limits, Sunday morning on the Brigsteer Road was strange to see. It is elevated with vistas toward the Howgills and the Yorkshire Dales, so here came dog walkers and all walkers dodging the traffic on this winding, undulating road and all looked wistfully toward the distant, forbidden hills. As spring progressed we made the most of the early purple orchids and cowslips of the grass verge. It was a time to take exercise exploring Kendal with its secluded yards and the possibility of avoiding traffic via the flights of steps of its western hillside whose layout reminds me of Italian hill towns. In May I scrubbed my walking boots with disinfectant for a trip to Umbria, with my friend David, although I hadn't worn them since the outbreak began.

The Foot and Mouth epidemic persisted longest in the Eden Valley and the Penrith Spur. On 1st August 2001 some new areas were opened to walkers, and a map with a network of promoted paths was published, but the Lake District was one of the last places to have the countryside ban lifted. Scotland was clear rather earlier and the Lochaber 2001 went ahead: six days of orienteering. We were asked to dip our orienteering shoes in a disinfectant bath near farm land but beyond that lay freedom. Two hours training beneath Ben Nevis and what a joy to slosh into bog and streamlets, seeing small pools half-hidden and deep in fragrant bog myrtle and reedy tussocks. Amongst bog asphodel and orchids streamlets were audible but often invisible, and my footsteps raised dark butterflies.

It was a disorientating time. I was in New Zealand at Christmas for an antipodean spring and then the English spring was lost and I felt dissociated from the seasonal rhythms I love. By late August I was back on the fells but with this strange feeling of the year having gone topsy-turvy.

The farmers were stuck on their farms throughout the epidemic and their diversification into bed and breakfast and teas was of no financial help because access to properties on farmland was debarred. It is impossible to imagine the hardships they endured during this time, and subsequently.

Interlude with books

2001 was a lost spring, a lost summer; a hiatus. There was an enforced absence from Scout Scar and the fells during the Foot and Mouth epidemic. If for any reason I can't be outdoors I turn to books, which have always been important to me. Coming home from a walk and an exploration, it's my habit to read up on what I've seen and to go out and look again. And so it goes on. As we were flying over the frozen landscapes of Finland, a young scientist confided his enduring love of birds that began in childhood. He chooses a field guide as bedtime reading and his wife doubts there could be more to learn from a book he's turned to many time before – 'You must know it all by now'. But you never do. It's a particular kind of reading.

Memories of books we read in childhood stay vivid. We pore over them, our young minds uncluttered and receptive, and we give our imagination free rein. My father loved to take me bird watching and his showing me a quarry cliff where sand martins nested and our watching swallows skimming a river is one of my earliest and fondest memories. We used to study the *Observer's Book of British Birds* and the *Observer's Book of British Wild Animals*, which I still possess and I look up hare, a Scout Scar special, to find the creature compared to a hermit. The leporine way, he wants to be alone.

How could it be that my Alison Uttley *Little Grey Rabbit* books were lost? They captured the magic and mystery of the dry stone wall with its sheltering habitat, its sanctuary of crevices, niches and internal runways.

Cicely Mary Barker painted her flower fairies in 1923 and I was nurtured on these illustrations. Hers are little akin to the dark and feisty fairies of Shakespeare's imagination. Her blackthorn fairy has the delicacy of the beautiful early flower that struggles to come to much on Scout Scar. Gorse is up there on

Gorse or furse, Ulex europaeus *and blackthorn*, Prunus spinosa.

the limestone and in strong sun its flowers give off a ravishing fragrance, rather like coconut mushrooms, a favourite childhood confection. Barker's poem begins with a line of folk-lore about kissing being in fashion only when gorse is blooming. Now *Ulex europaeus*, or furze, flowers throughout the year so kissing has an open season. Her fairies are about to kiss: the Bronzino kiss – almost, almost. (Iris Murdoch names the kiss after an erotic painting of Venus and her son Cupid almost kissing.) Prickles of gorse surround her fairies who seem heedless of hazard. At the touch of an insect the flowers explode, showering the pollinator with pollen. On a hot day the ripe seed pods explode in a fusillade of poppings: a dehiscent plant. Over time, this to and fro revisiting of beloved books changes and enriches them.

Books are a lifeline, a consolation and a solace to the ten year old Jane Eyre on a dismal November day when she shuts out Gateshead and loses herself in Thomas Bewick's *History of British Birds*. The volume she chooses is his *Waterbirds* in which Bewick is possessed by the thought of Arctic zones: the summer breeding grounds of his birds. The book has a powerful hold over the girl whose imagination is captured by Bewick as she delves his images and tries to understand the mystery, to fathom the story behind the engravings.

Thomas Bewick's engravings take you there. His two volume work (1797 and 1805) is an entrée to a landscape, to an England that is lost. For each bird there is an engraving, a scientific study followed by specific data. He finishes with a flourish, with a vignette minute and crammed with detail. He calls his vignettes tail-pieces or tale-pieces – they're stories that round off each entry. These are disturbing landscapes, there is darkness and malevolence abroad. Here is an England lost and not altogether regretted. There is the motif of the gibbet and birds of ill-omen come with obscure tales of violence: the long-eared owl prefaces a suicide hanged from a bough over a river; two ravens show an ominous interest in a hanged man on a gibbet; a devil lashes a man into position below the noose hanging from a gibbet; a cameo of a horned, winged and tailed devil with distant gibbet, in use, accompanies a beautiful engraving of the chatterer, the silk tail or waxwing.

In his *Waterbirds* these dark and cryptic tale-pieces were 'an object of terror' to Jane Eyre: the fiends, the gallows. And sailing ships on stormy seas of ice, in danger of wrecking on ice cliffs, and a flock of gannets flying low over the waves. Bewick is an ornithologist with startling flights of imagination. There is an early image where an explorer, like Icarus with feathered wings, is drawn toward the moon by a flock of white birds. His 'fancies', he calls these tale-pieces.

Bewick's birds were often autopsy studies. *Natura morta*, dead nature, the Italian is forthright. He does not adopt the *still life* convention but shows his birds resurrected in their habitat. Eighteenth century naturalists requisitioned the birds they wished to study. They had a profound love of the natural world but shooting came naturally; here was no ethical dilemma, they were of their time. Gilbert White, in his *Natural History of Selborne* (1789), felt that the sportsman's instinct ran deep. His journals record a gamekeeper's sending him a peregrine shot for taking a wood pigeon and, whilst in Gibraltar, his brother sent him 'dead specimens' of birds. Wheatear was regarded as a delicacy and White tells of shepherds making money from trapping them as the birds gathered on the South Downs. There were larkers out at night with nets and bat fowlers too. In April ring ouzels arrived, to be shot by White who dissected one, ate it and found it tasty. Out with his pointers after harvest, he shot stone curlews.

Responsive to seasonal movements of birds, White and his contemporaries debated migration but stopped short of endorsing the concept. He noted claims of hirundines appearing, as if roused from hibernation, on a warm day in early November. And he could not quite accept the inevitable loss of all those late-season broods of swallows and house martins, doomed to perish if migration were proved a reality. Avian journeys are awesome and White and his contemporaries balked at the concept, but it was more than a glimmer on their horizon.

In the late 18th century the day to day relationship of man with nature was immediate, intimate and sensory. Pigs might run around the farmer's wife as she hung out her washing. Bacon hung drying in the chimneys and flies laid their eggs in it. Other creatures had a taste for it too – was it bats? Owls fell down chimneys, perhaps in pursuit of swallow nestlings. There were harvest mice in the barns and ricks, and the barn door was adorned with trophies: a heron, albino rooks, and a barn owl caught taking squabs from the dove cot. House thatch wasn't sterile and great tits dislodged straws in their search for flies. Our twenty-first century homes tend to insulate us against the natural world; double glazing muffles the dawn chorus.

Throughout his life and from day to day, Gilbert White was immersed in looking about him, in studying and recording the natural world and always with a questioning spirit and a sense of wonder. His monographs on hirundines show the depth of his passion. In reading his journals there are moments when time dissolves in recognition of a shared experience and a shared excitement.

2002

June 2002: Scout Scar, the Mushroom Shelter

Blazoned *viewpoint* on the OS map, there you have it: the Mushroom Shelter.

On a clear day, the panorama is spectacular and the toposcope attracts walkers to get a fix on the Lake District Fells, Fairfield, Kentmere, the Howgills and the Yorkshire Dales. It is located at almost the highest point of the ridge at about 230 metres and you may see people making for it, being drawn to it. To those familiar with the place it is a focus of affection and nostalgia. It commemorates the Coronation of King George V in 1911 and local people have been coming to the Mushroom viewpoint on Scout Scar ever since.

The Mushroom Shelter was due for refurbishment, disfigured with graffiti and with chicken wire protruding from the cement within the dome. Its map is said to have been painted out during the second world war to foil German parachutists and had probably been repainted several times since its inauguration in 1912, so its accuracy was doubtful. In 2002 it was refurbished and all democratically done. We were asked whether we would like a new design or the status quo and the latter was the popular choice. The low Griffin step, to the south of the shelter, eases the ascent to the encircling stone seat. Harry Griffin contributed to the *Guardian Country Diary* for years and he was up there watching the refurbishment approach completion and, being 92, he requested *one small step* and the workmen were happy to oblige. The new stainless steel dome affords

Yew, Taxus baccata. Ripe, red yew arils whose black, poisonous seeds are visible within the sweet flesh. And whitebeam berries.

Birch trees high on the track which ascends the scarp slope from Barrowfield Farm. Whitebeam and yew show high on the buttress. 31.3.2008

shelter and was made by a specialist in Bradford who makes dome ends for milk tankers. David Silk's new map was engraved on a set of eight stainless steel sheets and fixed in position inside the skirt, allowing you to locate fells round about with considerable accuracy, using the central sighting rod. The four posts, main supporting pillars, give an exact position of the four cardinal points. The map takes you to the fells you aspire to climb, or to fells and routes you remember with pleasure. You may lock yourself into the landscape and look out upon the panorama to name what you see. You might play the Mushroom game in reverse by seeing if you can pin-point its domed structure from near and more distant eminences; from Lord's Lot, from Whitbarrow, from the hospice tower on Hampsfell, or from Bannisdale.

Since 1912 the market town of Kendal has grown considerably and pressure on the landscape is evident as the path along the escarpment edge grows wider and more worn, especially as paths focus on the Mushroom. I'm glad it was restored to commemorate the Golden Jubilee of King George's granddaughter, Queen Elizabeth II.

19 October 2002: Scout Scar. Looking into the escarpment

I set off for Scout Scar to see the frost effects in the landscape and to find fieldfare below the escarpment. A mass of illuminated fog marked the position of Windermere. Whitebeam were a glory of rich red berries, their leaves crisped after weeks of fine weather. And there were rich holly berries. The escarpment was deep in shadow but the sun began to catch and warm those steep pitches of limestone scree scattered with yew trees. Startled pheasants took off, cackling raucous. Something below the rock face tapped loudly, perhaps the nuthatch I had heard. Flocks wove silently amongst the dark yew with pale, glinting wings and the chacking call of fieldfare. A peaceful and glorious few hours alone along the edge of the escarpment as the activity of the wood below opened up to me.

A path from Barrowfield Farm winds its way up the escarpment to the cliff top where golden-green birch frame a fine view north toward Red Screes and Yoke. Sunlight depicted the fells so that the architecture of the mountains was revealed. Gable had a hint of cloud but all else was sunlight and shadow.

2003

3 May 2003: *Bradleyfield Allotment and Helsington Barrows*

Beyond Bradleyfield Farm, flowers abound. A cuckoo was calling, and having woken to a radio programme on cuckoo lore my head was full of their breeding habits and the precision timing needful if the female is to find a meadow pipit host and lay her egg in its brief absence from the nest. I set myself to track down this vocal male in open terrain with only a scattering of trees, so I had a good chance if I persisted. I skirted a field with several clearance cairns and it sat in the top of a hawthorn. This was the first time I had found a cuckoo for myself and that felt special. New lightweight binoculars were opening up opportunities, and I could home in on the fells too. There was good visibility today toward the Langdales from the viewing point of the Mushroom Shelter. It was dry until midday, then there was light rain as predicted.

On the National Trust land at Helsington Barrows there are Galloway cattle from the isle of Mull, recently introduced to promote the flora of this limestone grassland in a conservation project. They're dark and stocky with long, thick hair. They're said to be unused to people but today they strayed across the track and seemed indifferent, which suits me. Beyond the Helsington gate there is a roadside bank of cowslip and a few early purple orchid.

2004

3 February 2004: *a ghyll, Blind Beck and the River Kent*

The River Kent has a history of flooding in Kendal which is situated on a flood plain, and the confluences of its tributaries, the Sprint and the Mint, are just north of town.

There had been heavy, almost incessant rain for days and I put on my wellies and went into town to see the developing drama. I planned to track the course of a tributary full of character that rises close to home, an occasional beck which often lacks surface water because it cuts through permeable limestone. How would this beck respond to serious rainfall? It's a covert and secretive occasional watercourse but street names tell of its presence. The OS map reads *spring* then *sinks* just above Ghyll Brow. It crosses the Brigsteer Road in a dip prone to flooding. Hidden below Ghyllside School and Gillingate there is a spectacular feature where water had backed up behind a grill choked with debris and emerged from a culvert to plunge some forty feet into a secluded ravine where jets of water spouted from the limestone.

Now Blind Beck, it follows a channel between the houses of Anchorite Fields and Buttery Well Lane and the din gave away its course as it roared and battered its way down through Kirkland. The footbridge beside Abbot Hall was clogged with debris and the beck had flooded the flowerbeds. The River Kent raced by, brown, turbulent and having spilled over its banks so that access to Jenning's Yard Footbridge was under water. Logs and a window frame were swept along at a furious rate. Flotsam was dumped on the muddy grass and wavelets lapped a clump of snowdrops in a riverside garden. A young woman stood nervously smoking a cigarette and watching the rising water levels. She lived in a ground floor apartment by the Abbot's Hall children's playground and they had been warned they might be flooded out. I headed north, feet in the Kent overspill, past the wholefoods cafe by Miller Bridge where the women were putting sandbags in place. Flashlights were going off along the Kent as photographers made a record of the drama. There was an unsettling voyeurism as sightseers mingled with anxious home owners and I heard one woman say how beautiful it was. Gooseholm pedestrian bridge had been cordoned off by the police. Its access was under water and it appeared insubstantial in the furious river. Cars in a riverside carpark looked set to float. The weir below Stramongate looked terrifying and water raced violently below the piers of the bridges. I had never met so many Kendalians at a swoop and they were all eager to tell me how long they had lived here and how no-one remembered anything like this since the 1970s. Above

Victoria Bridge we could see and smell a slick of fuel and the contaminated water invaded the riverside cottages.

When I called in at Kendal Sports on my way home the men told me the river used to come part way up Finkle Street but had not done so since the 1970s when a flood alleviation scheme was put in place in response to serious floods in 1954 and 1968 and the Kent was made wider and deeper.

An image of the River Kent lingered in my mind: a dangerous, brown river powering through the town. The Kent is always a fast flowing river. Its source is in the fells about High Street at about 830 metres and in twenty miles it debouches into Morecambe Bay where it is notorious for its shifting channels.

Early in February, nineteen Chinese cockle pickers were drowned at night out in Morecambe Bay.

7 *February* 2004: *Kentmere*

We walked in Kentmere in a circuit above the reservoir almost to the source of the Kent. The settled snow had gone although we had a day of hail, snow showers and sunshine. There was little sign that the river had been so turbulent and in spate. The head-waters flowed clear over a stony bed, its waterfalls were good and it was almost too deep to cross.

8 *September* 2004: *Scout Scar*

Another beautiful day with a cloudless sky and excellent visibility. Low tide exposed the sands of the Kent estuary. Flies buzzed over fading heather. A crow was lit silver-white and swallows skimmed low over the escarpment, blue-black and glossy. Whitebeam rooted in the cliff face had green berries. There is a sunny place sheltered by hawthorn, where the merest hint of breeze just catches the cliff edge. Below, there is a dead yew whose form is swept by the prevailing winds toward the escarpment where steep grass meets limestone scree. Swallows glinted black and white and I began to see that its bare branches were full of fluttering swallows: a throng of birds. There was the hum of flies and the swallows were feeding up and mustering before the long flight to Africa.

Next day the yew was bare, not a swallow to be seen.

2 December 2004: Home and Helsington Barrows

A cold December morning with fog that the sun shot through, illuminated, and dispersed. Fog hung over the Kent estuary and showed up the course of the river and, from Scout Scar, the location of Windemere. Near the toposcope by St John's Church, I heard fieldfare come down into a cluster of intertwined holly and hawthorn. The highest branches were bare of leaves and holly berries glowed like red hot pokers. What an abundance of fruit. In the dense tangle of holly and hawthorn the fieldfare feasted, hidden until they flew with a glint of silvery-pale underwing.

Back home at midday I left off reading and went to post a letter. A flock of birds flew overhead. Were they starling? They came down in an exotic rowan but I couldn't focus: I was still wearing reading glasses so I ran down the road to change them, to grab binoculars and to hurry back. I suspected the birds were waxwing and I found myself praying for the chance to find out. I might have walked beneath a rowan full of waxwing and might never know for sure. How tantalising! Four years ago a solitary bird came after garden berries and sat sapped of vitality

Mist over the Lyth Valley, from above Burnbarrow Scar. 14.11.2007.

and colour on a dull day. Now as I walked into the sun there was a single bird perched on the topmost branch and I saw its crest in silhouette. Yes! There were more birds in the tall trees beyond the wooden, roadside fence: the unmistakeable silhouette of waxwing. Then the flock flew over me and fluttered down into the rowan rich in fruit. The light was perfect: strong sunlight full on them as they gorged on pannicles of pinkish-white berries on bright red stems against a blue sky. Acrobatic in feasting, every facet of the bird was caught in the sunlight: bright yellow bar on the tail feathers, brilliant pattern of yellow-white markings on the wing feathers, red wax spot beneath the wing, warm chestnut vent and jaunty cockade. Startling, this colourful plumage on these Scandinavian visitors at the onset of winter. The tumblers were come to town and they were ready to perform at the banquet. What an act! Hurrah for the tumblers. Colour and warmth suffused the birds, and me too. They fed and fed, oblivious of me. If a car turned into the road, frighted, they flew back into the birch trees. They returned to strip the last berries, then flew into the high trees and came no more. All of twenty minutes I had watched, wholly focused on this flock of more than thirty birds.

Next day, fog descended and rain set in. What good fortune to encounter a flock of waxwing on the one bright day of the week, wonders and marvels right here on my doorstep. The tree is a Hupeh Rowan native to China. Those red stems stuck up on their pannicles quite bare of fruit and I wondered how often a flock ventures to feed in gardens all unseen. There was a stripped Hupeh Rowan in my own garden. I wonder …

Four days later and the waxwing were abroad again and their second choice was a rowan with yellow berries. It was a Sunday morning and there were people outdoors chatting, with cars arriving and departing and the flock was easily disturbed. A little lad called out, 'look at all those birds!', but no-one heeded him.

Their migration into England can never be taken for granted. Theirs is not the predictable, seasonal coming of fieldfare and redwing, but there are waxwing winters and this was one.

Three years later, on Scout Scar, I met a couple from Cedar Grove who told me they had filmed this waxwing flock feeding on berries in their garden. I like this sharing of wildlife finds, this generous exchange of information on what to find and where, with just a hint of the competitive: 'I wish I had seen what you tell me of; not many people have seen that. If only I had the photographs!' It's a kind of community bonding, such appreciation.

2005

11 May 2005: *Bradleyfield Allotment and Helsington Barrows*

The light was strong and bird song filled the place. I had sometimes heard elusive linnet and today I had my first sure sighting up here. Where the Helsington Barrows gate opens onto Brigsteer Road the verge had early purple orchid, crosswort and a profusion of cowslip.

12 May 2005: *Bradleyfield Allotment and Ghyll Brow*

It was a perfect May morning, with sunshine from dawn, and I awoke with my heart set on linnet. On Scout Scar I heard them in flight and turned away from the escarpment thinking to find them where there is more gorse, and so it was. First a male in an ash tree sang lavishly. The joy of it! You are intensely in the moment, enhanced by linnet memories that come flooding back, like the spring of 1984 along the Gower coast, and Wormshead with linnet in breeding plumage. On Scout Scar you have to persevere to find linnet, they don't just present themselves as they often do along a coastal path walk. Today, linnet gave generously of themselves.

Having been out for hours I was passing Ghyll Brow, my excursion almost done, when I heard a high, piping sound. Was it a small mammal in the dense brambles? Above me were sycamore with the sun penetrating fresh, just-opening leaves in a golden glow and the piping came from within this foliage and it took a while to locate it, longer to make out what I was seeing as I was looking into the sun: long, black and white tails and a tumble of bodies, a brood of long-tailed tits. The fledglings were bundled up within the fork of a slender branch and both parent birds were busily filling their beaks with insects that were plentiful here in the sycamore and stuffing food into chicks that were so glued together that heads and tails were all a-jumble, as if they had been tight-packed within the nest and still clung together with no concept of personal space. At least six tails spiked that ball of hungry fledglings.

Home again, but this find was so special I quickly went back. A goldfinch with red face mask sang in an ash opposite my long-tails' sycamore, which was silent and empty. For the first time I noticed that the Ghyll Brow hillside pasture was white with what seemed to be lady's smock, just covered in it.

Heather above Scout Scar escarpment.

27 June 2005: Bradleyfield Allotment and Helsington Barrows

A lovely summer's day with strong sunlight that intensified colour. Everywhere there were small birds feeding their young; stonechat, pipit and a skylark that came down clear against the sky and into the heather. A jay gave an alarm call from larch trees and a pair of buzzards circled above me, their wings translucent. Perched on a hawthorn was a male linnet with the sun on its back and the sky as a bright blue foil. Deep, deep gold and singing away to its heart's content, and mine. It turned its pink breast toward me and sang on and on whilst the sun conferred upon it a depth of colour I've never seen before. How wondrously the sun makes and unmakes colour. It soared into my pantheon of celestial linnet, this golden bird.

There were rock rose on the escarpment edge and the flora of Helsington Barrows was responding splendidly to the Galloways' grazing. There was yellow lady's bedstraw among the white, St John's wort and drop wort with its pinkish buds and frothy white flowers on red stalks. Thyme flowers everywhere, with black and red burnet moths feeding on their nectar. Fragrant orchids in the grass, a fritillary on the path and colourful butterflies which came down into the grass, closed their wings and vanished.

There was a commotion down by the ghyll where a kestrel was being mobbed by jackdaw. The field was rich in buttercups and sorrel. A fat kestrel fledgling sat looking out from a niche in the stonework of the barn, and retreated to reappear with a sibling. All this within moments of home.

29 June 2005: *Scout Scar from Brigsteer*

It might seem rash to offer a friend linnet but this spring I was finding them every time as I knew the habitat they favoured and I knew their behaviour. I felt I was in on the secrets of the place. It was alive with birds calling to each other and busily feeding their young.

Irene and I descended through Barrowfield Farm and through the plantation where January storms had brought down huge trees. The grasses were in flower and what a variety! Goldcrest were in the tree tops. We heard green woodpecker and great spotted and saw both fly.

1 July 2005: *Scout Scar*

A breeze and cloud with some sun. Kestrel were abroad. Stunning, this image of raptor against the sky. A curlew was being seen off by corvids. Along the escarpment there was a hawthorn on which a pair of stonechat and a linnet shared my binocular frame.

9 July 2005: *Scout Scar*

A very hot morning with cloud cover by mid-afternoon. Fritillaries on the Scar. Slender St John's wort everywhere, with burnet moth. The first scabious were coming into flower. The kestrel nest was empty, merely bird shit to show where it had been. I discovered two brown blobs on the top of a wall close by the nest and the female flew in bringing food for her young.

18 August 2005: *Scout Scar and Helsington Barrows*

Kestrel was the bird of the day. Along the escarpment edge buoyed up by the stiff wind, seeking height, head focused on the ground, the bird fell and rose again. Then a second bird appeared and they drifted over the escarpment, ablaze with purple heather, and flew off together. Another came down in a larch on Helsington Barrows, its yellow legs and grey head clear to see. Close to the church, a pair of buzzards.

Ash rooted in clitter on the limestone ridge above Scout Scar. The wall marks the National Park boundary and a parish boundary: Helsington Barrows is to the right, Bradleyfield Allotment to the left. 31.3.2008.

19 August 2005: *Scout Scar and Helsington Barrows*

Glorious day with bright white clouds sunlit amongst the blue. By the gate onto the Scout Scar race course a breeze rustled the tall willow herb whose plumed white seeds were caught up into the air, whilst a bee fumbled the last of the fading magenta flowers.

Butterflies everywhere. And kestrel, hunting along the escarpment. How beautiful they looked against the luminous white cloud! An adult was teaching hunting skills to a juvenile. Ten sightings of kestrel but how many birds? In a larch with branches swaying and soughing in the breeze were several coal tits. From the high point of Helsington Barrows there was excellent visibility toward the Coniston fells and south to the Kent estuary.

To the trig point and down beside the dry stone wall en route for home when I heard an unfamiliar call and in a hawthorn over the wall I spied a pale-breasted, slightly speckled and dark grey fledgling with black beak and legs. Eliminating all that it was not, I knew it was special. More fledglings amidst the leaves were being fed beakfuls of insects by an adult bird with a rosy breast. At such times the thrill and the concentration of it suspend you out of time, yet the clock ticks relentlessly because at any moment the bird might dive deep into foliage, or fly off. At last, it flew with a flick of its scarlet tail: a female redstart, the first I have found here for myself. I walked home in the glow of the experience.

20 August 2005: *Scout Scar and Helsington Barrows*

On this hot and sunny day, the blue sky bright with clouds, the redstart family was a powerful lure. Butterflies chased each other in spiralling flights and flies were visible about the vegetation. The dry stone wall where I found the redstart family has soft, old curves and it sags and leans in a loose fabric of stones that provides a perfect nest site. The nearest hawthorn has a heart of old, gnarled branches and it forms a dense shield of thorn and leaves in a cluster of old trees, including a stout holly. Two smart wheatear appeared atop the wall which runs undulating toward the trig point. Sharp stones, sharp slats of limestone, cram together in a *mille feuille* effect. Topstones are loosely placed in seemingly random fashion: stones picked right up from the limestone clitter that is everywhere.

18 *September* 2005: *Scout Scar*

Overcast and cloudy, poor light. By the gate approaching Bradleyfield Farm there was a charm of goldfinch feeding on thistles that grew thick along the wall. On the ground and on swaying thistle heads they foraged, a fluttering of gold on the wings. The last few swallows perched on the wire beside a chestnut thick with spiky, ripe fruit.

27 *October* 2005: *Scout Scar*

The warmest on record! Butterflies on Scout Scar on a sunny, warm and hazy day. Leaves were slow to colour in the unseasonably warm weather but heavy rain and wind this last week had stripped hawthorn and whitebeam of their foliage. I heard and saw a few fieldfare and a kestrel huddled in a bare tree.

18 *November* 2005: *Scout Scar*

With bright sun on deep frost the woods were glorious. Winter birch was all silver bark and crowns of purple. Finding fieldfare and redwing has become a rite of autumn and I heard them moving through the wood as they stripped the fleshy red arils from the yew tree grove on the steep scree of the escarpment buttress. Trees below the escarpment were in the grip of sombre frost and on the western fringe of the wood, caught in sunlight, were tall birch outliers crowned with fieldfare amongst their last golden leaves. Some flew into the gloomy dimness of yew foliage and were lost to sight and a solitary fieldfare fed on yew arils in the sunlight. There was the chatter of mistlethrush and the softer call of redwing. Below me was the twisted and gnarled skeleton of the yew where swallow gathered last September before migration. Whitebeam growing in the cliff face were already stripped of berries and two silhouettes brought me to a halt. I knew the shape of the bird, that bulky head with a hint of crest. Waxwing. They fluttered and settled again with the sun now showing a little of their colour. Close to the cliff edge sat a couple who were looking out toward the fells and I asked if they would like to see waxwing. They thanked me but said 'they would be wasted on us'.

19 November 2005: Scout Scar

My friends Jane and Nigel came over from Kirkby Lonsdale eager to see waxwing. Fieldfare were in the high birch crowns and we heard redwing but of waxwing there was no sign.

21 November 2005: Scout Scar

The sea over Morecambe Bay was lost in mist and sunlight. It was much warmer and insects were flying. There was a buzzard beside my barn, and greenfinch. In the wood below the escarpment mistlethrush and redwing fed on yew arils. Fieldfare called as they flew and came down in those tallest trees on the further edge of the wood.

3 December 2005: From Brigsteer

Rain and another of those days when it is scarcely light before 10.00 am and darkish by 3.00 pm. We decided to go for a walk through Low Plantation, Barrowfield Lot and Honeybee Wood. Missing our way, we found ourselves clambering through brashings and through the branches of felled and fallen trees! There were woodpiles along the track and felling will have opened up the ground to flora. We found earth ball fungi, a pair of buzzards and great spotted woodpecker. It was Saturday and there was shooting in the wood.

Bedding planes in the carboniferous limestone of Scout Scar cliff face are visible, with dark slivers of yew in the rock. Whitebeam grows in the cliff and high on the buttress. The rare Sorbus lancastriensis *is a speciality of this location.* Sorbus rupicola *is also found here. The shape of the leaves and berries is definitive.* 10.4.2008

6 December 2005: Bradleyfield in-bye land

Today, there was sunlight blocked by a mass of cloud over Kendal and light struck obliquely through it. The sun was low and walking south into it made visibility restricted. On the race course pasture there were fieldfare and as the ground was so soft perhaps they were after insects and worms. A kestrel huddled in a tree as it was chilly. I saw birds in the top of a hawthorn, approached under the cover of a dry stone wall, and there amidst the winter-shrunken thistles was a flock of fieldfare foraging in the grass. The wall concealed me and the birds came so close. The light caught the rusty glow of their spotted breasts, sunlight conferring colour. Something frighted them and they flew. Further along the wall, in another field, more of them. A small flock of starling flew in and goldfinch perched close in a tree. Starling thrive alongside sheep and are often to be found in their pasture.

21 March 2006: *Bradleyfield Allotment and Helsington Barrows*

After the equinox, Finnish Lapland here I come. March continued unusually cold with a hint of snow in the air so I was out there trying my Arctic gear: a duvet jacket, bank-raider headgear and tall wellingtons, with a warm, red neoprene lining, which I planned to wear with three pairs of socks. As I walked up to the Scar a dozen curlew flew overhead and I heard the bubbling call I love: a sign of spring. Mucky snow had been pushed by a snow plough to clear the road by Helsington Barrows where the verge showed only a hint of new foliage and none of the coltsfoot that awaited warmer weather. Bradleyfield pasture was dark and muddy after the snow.

23 March 2006: *Scout Scar*

Deep frost and cold with some brightness. Kestrel in a tree near the barn. About fifteen curlew were calling as I approached the escarpment. There were ewes with lambs in the Barrowfield pasture. A tiny creature in a protective coat was struggling. Its mother nuzzled it and appeared to lick it until it raised its head. Its sibling suckled but as the frail twin tried to stand its legs buckled beneath it. Even the sibling seemed to be urging it on.

25–29 March 2006: *Above the Arctic Circle From Ivalo, Finland to Varanger Fjord, north-eastern Norway*

Perhaps reading Philip Pullman's *Northern Lights* prompted me to give my explorations an Arctic Circle emphasis this year, although northern landscapes have long held an allure that may have begun in childhood with Hans Andersen's *The Snow Queen*. So it's off to Varanger Fjord, kept largely ice-free by the influence of the Gulf Stream and a magnet for birds at the beginning of the breeding season.

Haari, our young Finnish ornithologist, was a twenty-first century Papageno with a tape to lure a response from birds and a hotline to birder friends. He drove us north through Finland alongside the Tana, the best fishing river in Norway, now frozen and with spectacular ice falls. We crossed the border and headed for Tana Bru hoping for gyr falcon, the most northerly of the breeding falcons. Our telescopes scanned the cliff crags, their niches and overhangs. There was a double pillar of rock blotched with orange lichen and topped with snow and upon it was a gyr falcon outlined in profile against a blue sky. A classic image of bird and habitat: a pair of breeding gyr falcons in early spring. Bird specifics and aesthetics all in one.

To be out before breakfast at Vardo called for hardihood. Fully kitted up against the extreme cold, I stepped outside the hotel at 7.00 am and driving snow struck me full in the face. The snow plough tipped its load into the harbour close by an old, timbered building where a noisy colony of kittiwakes had a long-established nest site on a ledge overhung with straggling grass, and a row of white heads showed as if snow-capped. A raft of mixed eider was beginning its courtship display. We had a trip on a fishing boat with just room enough for the nine of us and chunks of ice sloshed across the deck so if we crossed it we too went slithering. From our sheltered bay, we looked out to the forbidding waves of the Barents Sea as we headed toward the breeding cliffs of the snow-gleaming Hornoya Island, where shag with breeding crests lined up on a lower ledge. Through sunlight and snow flurries we watched colonies of guillemot, razorbill, puffin and kittiwake which had already chosen their nest sites on the cliff face. Something disturbed them and they took to the air in a shimmer of sunlight. There were black guillemot at sea, with their wonderful red webbed feet. Only 300–400 king eider, said Harri! I saw my first Brunnich's guillemot in flight, I'm told. And there were harp seal and harbour porpoise. Dark clouds gathered and soon we were watching a mixed flock of eider and saw them huddle together in raft formation as the wind whipped up the waves and a snow storm engulfed them and us. Then as the sun came out again they relaxed and strung out in a line.

The taiga, the boreal forest in Finland, was deep in snow and birds were hunkered down against the intense cold but sunlight on rime ice made the birch trees a work of wonder. And into this landscape there came a herald of spring: a black-bellied dipper splashed in a stream with ice-fretwork and in an instant a male appeared, mated with her and was gone. And sunlit ice prisms came shimmering, floating so slowly down from the sky, translucent lozenges of ice, scintillating diamond dust.

Dipping into Gilbert White long afterwards, I read of a severe frost in Selborne in 1784. On 10 December he saw 'bright sunshine', the air full of icy spiculae, floating in all directions'. Floating in free fall, that was what fixed it for me: it was precipitation, not rime from his high hedges. He puzzled over what he was seeing and I wanted to say to him just type in 'ice particles' and it's there on the internet: 'ice prisms' or 'diamond dust'. He was 64 and had never seen this before, nor had I. It's heart-warming to discover this wondrous shared experience. It makes for an intimacy that doesn't always come about with one's contemporaries.

I thought of Jane Eyre enshrined in her window seat with Thomas Bewick's *History of British Birds.* She muses upon this coast of northern Norway and the North Cape, 'the stormy Hebrides', and Spitsbergen. 'Of these death-white realms I formed an idea of my own', she tells the reader, whilst dreaming of 'farthest Thule'. Man may travel no further and reality must give way to imagination, Bewick tells his nineteenth-century reader. But Jane has just outlined my itinerary for 2006.

9 April 2006: *Brigsteer Park*

To Brigsteer Park where wild daffodils, violets and celandines bloomed. There was a fallen sycamore trunk covered in fronds of moss, scattered with oak leaves, and fruiting with scarlet elf cup. It's a fungus I love to find and it favours sycamore. There is dead wood habitat: brashings, branches of lopped timber and senescent trees designated to stand and die back slowly. Traditional coppicing made use of every scrap of timber and there was a thrifty tidying and clearing of the site. Now things are different and native honeysuckle is left to climb toward the light and flower and brambles growing around a hazel coppice stool will help to deter deer from browsing on new shoots. The second and third year after coppicing see the optimum resurgence of flora in the newly cleared embayments – when the canopy has been opened up either by coppicing or naturally after a storm which brings down trees. Hazel grows slowly on the limestone and struggles to re-establish itself. There are red deer on the mosses but hazel grows more quickly there and so has a better chance of regenerating. In Brigsteer Park there is an understorey of native hazel, hawthorn, blackthorn and guelder rose.

Snow fell on Red Screes and on the Coniston fells and, as we descended through the wood to Brigsteer, on us.

10 April 2006: *Scout Scar and Helsington Barrows*

Hats off to a glorious spring morning with a cloudless sky. Hats off and ears free to tune in to birdsong, at last. Frost in the grass and snow on the fells. Linnet were returned from the coastal regions to breed, and skylark and meadow pipit. From its perch on an anthill, silhouetted against the sun with its crest raised, a skylark ascended in a peal of song, its wings fluttering translucent in the sunlight. It was a morning of larksong and the distant bubbling song of the curlew. The Helsington Barrows coltsfoot were opened unto the sun, a mirror of sun-like faces.

10 May 2006: *Scout Scar and Helsington Barrows*

A beautiful warm day. Swallows were back at Bradleyfield Farm, swooping low over the pastures, feeding. Kestrel and buzzard were about. Early purple orchid and cowslip bloomed in the short grass of Helsington Barrows. In the mossy shade of trees and stone walls were wood sorrel and violet. From above the escarpment, I saw the flash of a white tail and a deer broke from the wood into a field, leapt a hedge, came up against a stone wall and sprang up and over it with what seemed merely the lightest touch of the top stones.

11 May 2006: *Bradleyfield Allotment*

A hot day with a cloudless sky and a hint of haze. A song thrush sang in the top of an ash and willow warbler and bullfinch were singing. There is a shallow terrace of outcropping limestone and there I found a pair of wheatear, returned to their breeding site.

12 May 2006: *Bradleyfield Allotment*

Atop a mound of limestone, in the favourite colours of Queen Elizabeth I, the handsome male wheatear was sentinel. On a gorse bush a male linnet sang, showing the subtle colours of his plumage and tiny bill.

21 May 2006: *Bradleyfield Allotment and Helsington Barrows*

Out at 8.15 am since rain was forecast, again, for midday. A morning of lark ascending and a fine view of a skylark in full song. Past the estate managers, those small, black Galloways introduced some two years ago to graze the limestone grasslands and promote flora. A cuckoo sang on Helsington Barrows somewhere in a group of larch and I followed the call through short grass with early purple orchid, cowslip and blue moor grass. On higher ground there are larch and Scots pine and fine views over the Kent estuary, but there was a cuckoo to locate and I followed wherever it led, up and down across dry valleys with deciduous trees until at last I saw my bird perched in the top of a larch. It flew west into oak trees and later I heard it down in the Lyth Valley.

On the bank by Helsington Church someone was getting to know the ropes of a hang-glider. There's a seasonal shift in the woods below the escarpment, a transformation. May woodland is full of creamy-white tree flowers and rowan and whitebeam gave the scree slopes a lightness and brightness. Everything was lush and fresh after a week of rain.

Descending toward the Bradleyfield pastures I passed a stonechat on a juniper. The new leaves of the tall ash were crisp clusters of deep, golden-green and the song thrush was singing with his accompanist of the season, the willow warbler.

At Ghyll Brow the hillside pasture was a profusion of white flowers and it came upon me that my last year's attribution was mistaken. The field was walled and wire-fenced but by the footpath I came close. 'You must never pick wild flowers,' says the man who murdered his wife, the eponymous Rebecca. And we uphold Maxim de Winter's maxim. Inexcusable with the advent of the digital camera, and mine confirms delicate meadow saxifrage.

The field banks steeply down to Brigsteer Road and so cannot be ploughed. It has been undisturbed pasture for years, during the time two generations of the Chapman family have tended it. A little fertiliser is put on the land once a year (phosphate, potash and a little nitrogen) and it is grazed by cattle and sheep. In July or August it is tidied up: nettles and thistles are topped and dead grass is removed and the 3–4 inch sward is left to regrow. It's an old-fashioned pasture of 'sweet, herby grass' and meadow saxifrage thrives on this regime.

24 May 2006: *Kendal Race Course*

What a wet week or more! I walked into Kendal, via Blind Beck in which there flowed surprisingly little water, and admired the goosander which are often to be found on the River Kent. My journals were to be a book: I was defining the range and scope of it. At Henry Roberts' bookshop we drew up 1:10,000 maps to my personal specification. The shop was the sixteenth-century town house of the Bellinghams of Levens Hall and I was shown the dark, carved fireplaces and a

Scout Scar escarpment. The breaking buds of whitebeam have a whiteness about them and the undersides of its leaves show whiteness too: so the white tree.

cupboard with B for the Bellingham family and the date 1774 upon it and I heard tell of ghostly footsteps climbing the stairs.

On a cold and breezy afternoon I set out for a walk, although I came to a halt at the race course: 'Training gallop' states one OS map. An all-terrain vehicle stood with lights flashing and the field had been cleared of sheep. It transpired that a royal helicopter was about to land to collect the Duchess of Gloucester, who is president of the RNIB and was here in Kendal in that capacity, and the Bradleyfield farmers were waiting to meet her. Having been presented, they descended from the helicopter which took off with a swirl of air turbulence which whipped up a tissue that a lady-in-waiting had let fall. 'Oh dear, she's dropped the royal hanky,' said a voice beside me. Brian Bowness is a grazier at Bradleyfied and I was to learn that he has a flair for one-liners.

The writing enterprise was fresh and new and I was charged with creative energy and eager to hear about my chosen location, so this encounter was most opportune. It opened up a dialogue with those who work this land and Tony Chapman's family have farmed hereabouts through several generations. We were sharing wildlife finds and nest sites and he told me some people come down off Scout Scar and say there's nothing up there. Local farmers work in close conjunction with Natural England to meet conservation objectives so such a response is discouraging. In fact it's a Site of Special Scientific Interest and an Environmentally Sensitive Area and it's teeming. After some two hours of chat I walked home realising that here were dimensions that my future journals should explore. There was so much more I wanted to learn.

27 May 2006: *Bradleyfield Allotment*

Driving home from a Kendal Naturalists meet, I saw Tony Chapman approaching the track to Bradleyfield Farm, pulled up beside him and jumped out. Unsurprisingly, he looked surprised. And somewhat puzzled. It was hard to say just what I wanted. (I learn most when I leave someone scope to range in thought where they will.) He intended to walk Bradleyfield Allotment in search of a sick ewe and suggested I might accompany him. He has a farm just east of Kendal, off the limestone, and he told me how different farming is because of this different geology. Water supply has always been a problem for farms on the limestone where the hydrology is complex: on occasion water might surface, only to sink underground again. In one of the fields just above Bradleyfield Farm the OS map shows a disused reservoir where they caught water and piped it down to a trough to water cattle. And beside the farm is a dew pond which fills or dries up as the weather determines. His grandfather's brother farmed at Stainbank Green, then at Bradleyfield which used to be called Fisher's

Tenement. He was born at Bradleyfield House. So he knows intimately that patchwork of fields between these two farms; the in-bye land. On behalf of his aunt, his sheep graze Bradleyfield Allotment: higher, more exposed ground with rough grazing. There is more hawthorn than he remembers as a boy and earlier this spring I had seen them out there clearing and burning it to improve grazing for his sheep and to keep it open for flora. There is a delicate balance in what suits birds, what flowers. Natural England advises on the grazing, on control of invasive species like cotoneaster, and the condition of native species like juniper. As a boy, he helped mow bracken which was used as bedding for cattle, fertilised the grass outside the field network and planted and thinned out turnips on his knees.

Venture into the hinterland which is Bradleyfield Allotment, the limestone scrub east of the escarpment proper, and landmarks tend to disappear as you find yourself crossing dips and hollows that disorientate. You can get lost here. There are a couple of old footpaths, one of which leads from Barrowfield Farm to Kendal, but stray off those and you're on ground that is rough underfoot, with limestone clitter and a few sculpted fragments of limestone pavement. A hare jinked away over a shallow juniper slope and rocky ground and he told me he sees one most days when he is out here tending his sheep.

He showed me a boulder known as the Blue Stone which overlooks Bradleyfield Farm and the land his family have farmed. Once it bore a plaque which commemorated his grandparents, James Chapman 1891–1985 and his wife Lydia 1901–1987. At his grandfather's request his ashes were scattered here and the plaque was affixed to the boulder but it was ripped off and now lichens encrust the sculpted letters. To locals, to the hound trailing community, it's a landmark. It's visible from the Brigsteer Road, if you know just where to look.

The limestone clitter has its own flora of wall rue, herb robert, limestone fern, wood sage and strawberry. Next day I discovered delicate rue leaved saxifrage. This is a zone of spiny shrubs, everything on the spectrum of spiny, variations on a spiny theme. And it's May and they're all flowering: gorse a blaze of yellow with flowers whose fragrance reminds me of coconut mushrooms; holly with white against its evergreen foliage; abundant hawthorn and juniper. Bash a branch of juniper and clouds of pollen rise from the flowers that lurk beneath its spines. These shrubs make excellent cover for wildlife and he showed me a fox's den. There's blackthorn grazed hard and low to the ground, tiny knots of it on frost-shattered limestone. Nothing achieves much height here and within the limestone clitter plants are ground-hugging. Stunted is all some of them will ever make without standing water, on poor soil and on the exposed dip slope.

During the Foot and Mouth epidemic they had to find new lambing fields because of restrictions on movement of livestock. Wildlife flourished that year, birds and flowers did well because they were undisturbed. There were skylark everywhere. A dog-free season was beneficial to ground nesting birds and to the hare which they sometimes chase. Limestone clitter is a sheltering habitat for wildlife but it has a fascination for people who like to build walls and shelters. Scout Scar is within easy reach of Kendal, and so vulnerable to the impact of people and their dogs.

Swallows swooped through open doors in the farm barns to their nests about the rafters and being shown the interior of the barns was a treat. The rookery by the farmhouse has been in use through several generations. The pied wagtails make a nuisance of themselves by pecking at wing mirrors when the farmers park beside the barns.

21 June 2006: *Scout Scar and Helsington Barrows*

On the longest day with a forecast of storm-force winds, David and I set out for Scout Scar and into the assault and battery of the winds. The Bradleyfield swallows were not flying, nothing was flying. There was no perceptible shelter at the Mushroom Shelter, it's exposed up there. We turned down into the shelter of Barrowfield Wood with its tall trees, its honeysuckle and dog's mercury; such a contrast to the limestone scrub above the escarpment. From Barrowfield Farm we climbed up the wooded escarpment over ground strewn with white stars of guelder rose blossoms brought down in the gale. To Helsington Barrows where it is the season of dropwort, lesser butterfly orchid and mouse-ear hawkweed. Heavier rain set in and we donned waterproof trousers beneath a majestic oak, and in a low bough we discovered a slit in which David suggested we might post letters. A note of whimsicality. And that sufficed for exploration on such a stormy day.

Guelder-rose, Viburnum opulus, *on the scarp slope above Barrowfield Farm.*

26 June 2006: *Scout Scar, Bradleyfield Allotment and Helsington Barrows*

There was cloud cover and a light wind but it was all happening out on Scout Scar. Parents were busy feeding and nurturing, with young things filling out. The generation of summer 2006 presented itself. This was the annual parade of the juveniles, soon to resemble their parents but not quite there yet, although on the race course field there were fat, juvenile rooks as big as adults and still food-begging with wide open gapes.

Since 11th May I've watched my wheatear family as they reared three young and fed amongst rocks, buttercups and thistles and dags of sheeps' wool.

Above juniper and gorse, swifts were feeding low in great parabolas of flight and in their midst a kestrel hovered, dived, and moments later flew up with a small mammal in its talons.

Approaching the trig point, I was listening to a skylark and kneeling to a fragrant orchid when a wheatear with a juvenile called from atop a stone wall, and high in a hawthorn a stonechat with a beak full of goodies called, and a pipit perched close beside me. I had never seen so many stonechat up here. They're easy to locate from their insistent call and their habit of perching on the top of a wall or on the highest branch. Birds were calling everywhere, beaks full. The place was so alive and summer abundance was the keynote. Swifts and swallows were

Limestone fern, Gymnocarpium robertianum, *growing on limestone clitter. A fern both native and rare.*

The parkland habitat of Helsington Barrows with colonies of anthills on south-facing slopes of the limestone grassland. 29.4.2008

calling all along the escarpment edge. There was a soundscape of seasonal refrains and I like to be attuned. All the birds of Bradleyfield and Helsington make up the music of an English summer's day.

Mistlethrush made a clamour in treetops on Helsington Barrows as I climbed toward the highest conifers, making a digression through deciduous trees in a dry valley. Passing close to a sycamore, I heard a strange noise and stopped to listen. Two branches abutted just above my head, masking a neat hole in the hollow trunk of the tree: someone's well-fashioned front door, and this someone was at home. Listening close, I could hear a chuntering and churring within. Green woodpecker, I reckoned. I often hear one calling hereabouts. The hole was perfect woodpecker and something was making a weird noise so I knew what it was not. I couldn't stand so close to a nest hole without unsettling the parent bird, so I had to be content with the excitement of my find and move on. Close by, there were fritillaries feeding on thyme flowers and I stooped for the sweetest strawberry and a butterfly diversion.

29 June 2006: *Bradleyfield Allotment and Helsington Barrows*

I had to go back, of course. I had to revisit my woodpecker's tree hole, if that's what it was. I have to know. So I invited Irene to come with me to Helsington Barrows.

There was strong sunlight with a few white clouds, but if there's a breeze anywhere the escarpment edge usually catches it and it's pleasant even in the heat. A kestrel hovered where mine had killed, sunlight illuminating the markings on its spread tail where a feather was missing. There were fragrant orchid and the sound of grasshopper as we ascended toward the trig point, following the dry stone wall that marks the boundary of the National Park where the parish of Bradleyfield within meets Helsington without.

Within the enclosed parkland of Helsington Barrows lay the putative woodpecker's nest site. I heard a green woodpecker and saw it alight in a Scots pine. This area is made up of the wooded dips and hollows of dry valleys with higher ground affording vantage points over the Kent estuary. Yesterday, I had meandered across country and whilst I could visualise the tree in its immediate setting there were more trees and young bracken than I remembered. Our footsteps raised butterflies and moths before us and there were fritillaries everywhere and burnet moths that fed on thyme nectar. And strawberries to divert us. Where was that sycamore? The adult woodpecker called again, close by. It flew, and called from a larch and I saw a rock slope on the edge of trees and knew the contours were right. There was my hollow tree so I sneaked up and listened at the forked trunk. Silence. But from the tree hole a beak protruded briefly, and was gone. We moved off and found a place under nearby trees where we could sit in the shade and see without being seen by the adult, we hoped. A perfect English summer's day with dappled light on foliage which rustled in the breeze, and the hum of insects. A head looked out from the nest hole, and withdrew. Moments later it appeared again: dark looking beak and red on the crown. Gradually, the fledgling became a little more bold and leaned further out and we could hear its bizarre call, not yet the language of the adult woodpecker which replied but did not approach. Not wanting to disturb them, we moved on through delicate St John's wort, through creamy-white bedstraw, yellow lady's bedstraw, pink squinancywort, dropwort with its pink buds and frothy white flowers, through fading butterfly orchids and a single fading tway-blade.

Ants and their grubs are a favourite food of the green woodpecker and the calcareous grassland of Helsington Barrows is patterned with thick colonies of anthills with a flora of thyme, limestone bedstraw, bird's foot trefoil and fairy flax. Something had been delving, burrowing into them, flipping off a lid as if it were a trapdoor. It must be the Galloway cattle which were introduced because their way of grazing is good for flora as they break up the vegetation which makes holes for seeds to germinate. There was also rabbit damage – there were droppings and excavations but a rabbit could not slice off an anthill mound. Nor could badger.

We sat in the sun by the trig point and the parish boundary wall came alive with a parade of juveniles and their parents. Juveniles of this parish. There's a phrase in early parish registers: 'ye supposed son of, ye supposed daughter of'. With some juveniles you can only tell to whom they belong when they appear alongside parents, or food-begging. First stonechat and pipit. Moments later, a wheatear family of six perched on the top of the wall which ascends in an irregular curve, birds in harmony with the creamy-greys of the stones and outlined against the blue sky. And there were mistlethrush with beaks full of food. The English dry stone wall is a boon for bird watching this time of year, when foliage is dense.

2 July 2006: *Scout Scar and Helsington Barrows*

A blue-grey haze took out distant views. There were blue butterflies and fritillaries in the long, seeding grasses, sedges filled with the sound of grasshopper, insects buzzing and skylark singing. There were tormentil and the first scabious. On the escarpment edge, above Barrowfield Farm, there was a hint of breeze. The sun was blazing off the limestone and kestrels were using the thermals to hunt along the cliff edge. Dark red helleborine racemes had been nipped off before they could flower. They were shaded by conifers thronged with buzzing flies or growing on limestone clitter and exposed to the intense heat. Swallows were lively and vocal over the Bradleyfield barns and in the surrounding trees. At 8.30 am there were a few runners but by late morning there were people lying in the sun and sheep lay fagged and panting along the dry stone wall, too little shade to go round, their drinking trough filled to the brim.

4 July 2006: *Bradleyfield Allotment and Scout Scar*

My wheatear family was in situ, camouflaged amongst limestone. Two fledglings flitted about in play, like butterflies. There was just enough breeze to tremble the rare hoary rockrose of the escarpment edge. The fragrance of wild roses was in the air and the strong scent of bracken.

6 July 2006

7.10 am. Mist over Kendal after last night's violent thunderstorm. Humid, with foliage wet from the rain. Swift screeching in flight. Two fat kestrel fledglings sat side by side in their nest hole, dribbles of shit on the stonework below.

11 July 2006

7.10 am. The air was fresh and the sun bright. There was an early runner abroad and a boy walking his young spaniel. For over a week I had been watching a kestrel nest with three fledglings. The female sat for over two hours in a niche, flattened against

masonry and full in the sun. A fledgling ventured onto the steep-pitched barn roof and teetered, flapped his wings and was almost airborne, then scrabbled at the stonework of the vertical wall and somehow hauled himself back into the nest hole. At midday two of them were out on the tiles coloured with orange lichen and worn into a slightly sagging, several-slates-askew old roof. About Bradleyfield Allotment harebell and scabious were budding. Skylark were singing and stonechat were abundant.

13 July 2006: *Scout Scar*

The sinuous Scout Scar escarpment. Bottom left: a dead yew tree shows the effect of the prevailing south westerly winds. Slivers of yew grow in the cliff face.

Swallows fed low over the Bradleyfield pasture. A green woodpecker was probing its bill into the long grass, then it climbed an ash and showed its reptilian profile. A morning of blue butterfly. A grasshopper jumped, all green of body and wings. Their cryptic colouring is so effective that unless they move they are hard to see.

A kestrel was out hunting. My kestrel fledglings took their first, short flight down from an ash tree onto their roof.

Approaching the Mushroom Shelter, I saw a sudden movement as a lizard basking on a sun-heated fragment of limestone shot away into the clitter beneath a hawthorn.

It was a lovely morning but skylark and pipit were silent: their season of singing at an end. Raven called as they flew along the escarpment edge. Stonechat were vocal and my wheatear family were there amidst flowers and limestone.

14 July 2006: *Bradleyfield Allotment*

Not so stifling as the summer's day on which Mrs Yeobright met her death in Thomas Hardy's *Return of the Native*. Blue butterfly, fritillary, and grasshopper chirruping. A perfect day. Hot sun tempered by a breeze and a hint of cloud. Looking into the flowers beside the rocky path, I stopped and stared at an adder which disappeared into the bracken. My thoughts on that fatal day on Egdon Heath and Clym Yeobright cutting furze, I listened to fuzzy brown gorse pods exploding in the sun.

30 July 2006: *returned from Svalbard to Scout Scar*

Once more into the Arctic Circle, and I am come home from the Svalbard voyage possessed by all that I've seen and experienced: the solitude, the awesome beauty and daily witness of the struggle for survival in such an extreme environment. Watched barnacle goslings destined to winter at Caerlaverock, Solway, had not an arctic fox picked them off one by one and fed them to her cubs. Watched reindeer on a glacier pink with algal bloom whilst Brunnich's guillemot grunted on their cliff ledge, and a chick swam after its parents making a whistling call, and our zodiac drifted silently amongst bergy bits. Surrounded by walrus off Sjuoyane, islands at almost 81 degrees north. Watched polar bears skinning a seal and making a meal of blubber on the ice-floes surrounding our ship: so close we heard the ripping and chomping and had a close-up of bearded seal anatomy, its innards like knitting wools. Three big male ice bears red with gore, the attendant ivory gulls drinking in an icy pool of blood and yet immaculate. Two freshly killed seals for fifteen bears; for the aggressive males who shared a kill but saw off females with cubs. Heard a cub roaring as it swam after its mother through the ice floes, hitched a ride on her back, fell off and clambered back aboard as she dived into the water once more. Even Rinie Van Meurs, our exceptional Dutch naturalist and leader of over a hundred Arctic expeditions, had only ever read of that: it must be destined for his next book. During the six-hour polar bear picnic we were in the midst of the action.

East of the Austfonna ice cap, we sailed in uncharted waters through blue ice bergs and bergy bits broken off from the massive ice wall that our Russian captain told us had receded 750 metres in two years. Waterfalls cascaded the 40 metres of the ice-cliff: there were spectacular caverns where jets and arcs of water powered down from on high and burst forth from within the ice and I pondered silently on *Kubla Khan,* and Alph the sacred river, and caverns measureless to man, when a voice at my ear said, 'this makes me think of Thames Water and leaks in the system.' We were looking at the same ice cave and imagination took us in such different directions.

How do we relate to landscape and the natural world? After Svalbard?

Today there were well-defined clouds, bright sun, a west-south-westerly breeze that came whistling over the Scout Scar escarpment and soughed through the larch. A pair of ravens called and a buzzard mewed in the distance: soundscape of English summer birds, with grasshoppers. Blue butterflies were diverse as the shades of harebells in full bloom amongst scabious and purple thistles. A loping hare topped the escarpment and disappeared into the limestone and the golden seeding grasses and the just-about flowering heather. I shared a moment's appreciation with a runner as it flashed between us. Here, I find things for myself and not courtesy of Rinie of the Arctic. It is gratifying to make one's own discoveries, to make connections and to build up a sense of how everything comes together in a landscape one knows and loves. And the Arctic experience intensified the quality of this my English summer and made me see it afresh.

In Svalbard, we were seeing climate change. We could sail freely around the Svalbard archipelago because the summer pack-ice was gone, which bodes ill for the ice-bears. All this is being monitored by scientists at Ny Alesund where the barnacle goslings were eaten and cached by arctic fox cubs. The tundra flora on the west coast of Spitsbergen was unexpectedly past its best. How goes phenology here? Are things already failing to coincide in the way they have done in the past?

Back on Scout Scar and on the fells there was evidence of extreme July temperatures with grass burnt wherever rock has roasted it. The rhythm of the seasons is deeply ingrained in me. I love being locked into the patterns of the natural world. So the mood is elegiac as climate change sees us heading into uncharted waters.

3 August 2006: *Bradleyfield Allotment and Helsington Barrows*

Despite several days of heavy showers the ground looked parched, the grasses burnt. There were bright rowan berries, rosy green berries on guelder rose, green berries on whitebeam and juniper, and thick clusters of green rosehips and green sloes.

On Helsington Barrows there was a nuthatch and a goldcrest in the larch trees. A distant green woodpecker called. Flies basked in the sun on tree bark and butterflies were all about the glade. Two painted ladies fluttered along the escarpment, their thistle food plants were in flower and in the short grass there were carline thistles. A male stonechat had a fat caterpillar in his beak. All along the path through the bracken I was hearing a familiar call until a redstart perched on the top of the dry stone wall.

4 August 2006: *Bradleyfield Allotment*

Path-side flora was subtle rather than showy: yellow lady's bedstraw, eyebright, tormentil, harebell and scabious. And an insignificant-looking, exciting find. Frog orchid in the spot where I was seeking felwort.

Within the in-bye land of Bradleyfield Farm is a discrete habitat favoured by birds. There are mature trees within a field wall, itself a perfect nesting place because the slats of limestone are irregular with spaces between. And there is the dense cover of juniper, often entangled with rose and bramble, on the Bradleyfield

Allotment. Hearing a high-pitched piping , I put my ear briefly to the stones to confirm fledglings within. Atop the wall an agitated wren – it was her brood of young troglodytes within the recesses of stone. There was a robin with young, greenfinch, and amongst green sloes, a willow warbler. I had a long, close view of spotted flycatcher as it perched amongst the branches of an ash. I used to dismiss August as difficult for bird watching because there is so much foliage and so many juveniles but watching this spot throughout the summer has been a rich experience. I was out and about on Scout Scar, always with binoculars and eager to make discoveries, to find things.

14 August 2006: Bradleyfield Allotment and Helsington Barrows

There was a buzzing of insects about the late summer grasses in a landscape that had a dried-out look about it. Heather was flowering: an acid-loving plant which grows in the bands of soil in limestone hollows, loess deposited after glaciation or blown in from Morecambe Bay.

Felwort was budding, sometimes growing on the rocky path. In the trees close to Bradleyfield Farm, a juvenile willow warbler was flitting about upon the face of the stone wall in search of insects. And the spotted flycatcher family was most confiding. They sat on exposed branches; dark bill, dark legs, a dark eye and distinctive pale spots on the flank of a juvenile which opened its beak to reveal a startling orange gape as its parent offered an insect. When I turned to leave it called so insistently it seemed churlish not to stay and give it my full attention.

21 August 2006: Bradleyfield Allotment and Helsington Barrows

The Bradleyfield pied wagtail were about. A sweet smell of hay, baled and barned, drifted from the cluster of farm buildings. Goldfinch in ash. Horse chestnut laden with spiky green fruit.

Heather was resplendent and fragrant too. It was the season of purple and blue flowers: heather, scabious, harebell and felwort. There were random squirts of fruit jelly on the ground where birds had deposited seeds they had eaten and coated in nutrients, and there were tiny rowan seedlings that had been distributed in this way.

The rain was over and gone. The skyscape was dramatic with layer upon layer of Cumulus: gleaming white clouds against indigos and soft greys. It was raining over Arnside but above me there was blue sky. It was a day of clarity and the fells showed forth in sunlight and shadow and the Howgills were deep and dark.

24 August 2006: *Bradleyfield Allotment and* *Helsington Barrows*

A fine morning with clear blue skies and on a seed-distributing breeze there was sunlit thistledown. A juniper tangled with green rose hips and blackberries that tasted sweet, sour and earthy.

A pair of ravens flew so low overhead that I heard their wing-beats. A male kestrel flew up from the grass and perched in a hawthorn close by and we stared each other out. Several hours later there was a dead shrew attracting flies on the path. All that hunting gone to waste! He must have dropped the shrew, or abandoned it, on my approach.

Over toward Burnbarrow Scar there were two buzzards flying together, perhaps an adult teaching a juvenile. A kestrel glided on the wind along the escarpment edge. Beyond Barrowfield Farm, felling has left scars on the landscape. In the fields below a farmer drove a tractor over a ploughed field and white clouds billowed all about him and he deposited a whitish layer on the turned earth. Is it lime to fertilise?

On Helsington Barrows there were birds flitting about in sycamore and ash and the jizz said spotted flycatcher: juveniles chasing each other and coming to rest on bare branches. It was an insect-rich day, especially over heather, and there was abundant food.

There is a stand of larch where a nuthatch probed under flakes of bark along a dead bough and playful goldcrest were easy to see. I fell into conversation with a couple who were walking a labrador puppy, a guide dog for the blind in training. The man told me that three years ago there were cross bill in these larch, through which the wind made a sussuration like the sound of the sea and a green woodpecker called in the distance. Autumn gentian were flowering, with both purple and white flowering plants.

26 August 2006: *Bradleyfield Allotment*

Whatever it was ate twenty of them. Kernels in a mess excreted on the stony path.

Perhaps it was wild cherry, that indicator of earlier spring and climate change. There were purple-white sploshes of bird lime about.

It was a day of cloud and the landmark of Pike o' Stickle was swallowed up in mist. A flock of rooks made its way slowly along the escarpment edge, bombing a kestrel, foraging about the crags and flying south. Here was felwort, or autumn gentian, right on the stony track. No need to leave the paths to find the best of the flora.

Swallows fed low over the pasture and twittered in little groups along the barn ridge of Bradleyfield and starling lined up on the wires whilst the pied wagtail family was busy and vocal.

4 September 2006: Bradleyfield Allotment and Helsington Barrows

A robin sang in the quietness of early autumn. Puff balls along the path to the escarpment, dark spores ready to gush into the wind. There was a thrilling cloudscape pierced with light: bright altocumulus in spectacular configuration and a swathe of brooding darkness. Flood water gleamed in the Lyth Valley. Ravens and a kestrel patrolled the edge. Swallows flew wind-swept over the escarpment in glints of white and were caught in dark silhouette.

6 September 2006: Bradleyfield Allotment

About the escarpment there were swallows, with ravens whiffling in the wind, tumbling, twisting, turning, plunging.

Another rainy morning with a humid afternoon and the bounty of the season showed forth in an outbreak of fungi; the earth seethed. Ink cap, *Coprinus niveus*, in clusters on cow dung. Coprophilous fungi, dung-loving. Spores are consumed by grazing cattle, pass through the gut, are excreted, germinate in dung and fungal fruit bodies appear. Below larch, there were beautiful larch boletus with lemon pores and chestnut cap. I found one perfect in form. Often they're broken, sodden and worm eaten. In the pastures by Bradleyfield there were delicate *hygrocybe*, all waxy yellow and reddish. An outstanding year for fungi.

10 September 2006: Scout Scar and the Lyth Valley

The fells were blotted out in the haze. In the stillness, sound carried. Mid-morning was peaceful and I sat looking out over the escarpment edge contemplating the nearer view. Whitebeam were laden with fruit, their leaves green and autumn-blotched with colour, their fat green berries taking on rosy colour one by one. From the canopy below the cliff came intermittently the harsh cries of a jay and the sound of a nuthatch and swallows twittered above. A red admiral came down in the heather that faded into subtle colour. The overlooked and understated Lyth Valley; walking above the escarpment there's a tendency to look toward the tops, eminence to eminence. The toposcope encourages it, with its map showing an outline of the horizon and pin-pointing well-known fells. That's what is immediately attractive: to identify summits and to track routes you have taken or might take in the future.

Today the fells were invisible and something caught my eye across a cluster of fields down below in the Lyth Valley. Beyond Barrowfield Farm, beyond Honeybee Wood with its area of felled plantation, there are green pastures with a few sheep and outcrops of limestone. I could make out the grassy embankments of Underbarrow Pool with its sequence of bridges and Moss Lanes. Then came parallel lines and encircling curves that made bold patterns seen from 220 metres above and two kilometres distant. In the nearest field two tractors worked their way slowly and in tandem and obliterated dark strips as they passed, leaving a golden background. The blue tractor was fitted with a red forage harvester that sucked up the line of cut grass, chopped it into pieces in its rotating drum and shot it into the green silage container of the accompanying tractor. When the container was full they parted and a second green container and tractor came in to take its place. The tractor with container full of silage rattled along Third Moss Lane, disappeared in trees and unloaded at Tullythwaite Hall before returning. A flock of gulls foraged about the three fields where the farmers were taking advantage of the fine weather to make silage which would be fed to dairy cattle as winter fodder to boost their milk yield. Poor weather had delayed for a week this third cut of the season and the farmers were hard at work, whilst midday on a Sunday is playtime up on Scout Scar.

Let work meet play, conflate time a little, and the scene resembles a Breughel painting: *Childrens' Games* meets *The Fall of Icarus,* say. Soaring on a thermal are three para-gliders like airborne insects with colourful wings. And a leisurely hot air balloon. In the distance, a blue tractor and a red forage harvester work the patterned fields. From the direction of Cunswick Fell the hounds come yelping, toward the open scrub where orienteers study their maps to distinguish a marked cairn from a house that children built. Up on Scout Scar, walkers stride out whilst families with children picnic. Men here to commemorate a departed friend clasp each other in an embrace and one of them raises a vessel on high and flings its contents about the Mushroom Shelter: 'ashes to ashes'. A Welsh Black might be caught in the act of depositing life-giving dung from which sprout fungi that a figure kneels to photograph whilst someone else pours white powder into a trail of cow pats! Very Breughel, this coprophilia. On the stroke of noon the mystery is explained. There is a clatter of limestone clitter and runners come hallooing, with contact calls and the trail of white markers in cow dung to make sure no-one is lost. Down they go, out of sight into the trees below the cliff edge and onto the track down to Barrowfield Farm and soon the front runners emerge from the trees, clang the farm gate and put the pheasants to flight. At the end of the line comes a walking runner with a mobile phone to his ear, here but elsewhere, intent on his conversation so that he misses the turn off so perhaps he isn't with them. All the gear and no pace at all. As the runners clear the trees you might hear their footfall. Then they are gone and Barrowfield Farm, with its distinctive Westmorland chimneys, is peaceful once more. A Breughel is crammed with figures, so let's pack in more Scout Scar moments: children fly a kite or lug limestone to build a fortress or declare they're never going on another walk again – ever! A dog chases a hare and a farmer berates the man who set it on to chase a wild creature or let it terrify his sheep. A figure backs away from the cliff edge with vertigo, another dangles her legs over the cliff although she has chosen a spot where the edge descends in shelves and she might roll over but it isn't sheer. And folk make for the Mushroom magnet to rest (not all in perpetuity), to climb all over it, to picnic, to paint or to name fells.

12 *September* 2006: *Bradleyfield Allotment*

Another very warm and sunny day with cloud cover. On the path to Bradleyfield Farm was a family of pied wagtail with sooty juveniles. Swallows preened on the wire, put to flight by the arrival of starlings, then in came a charm of goldfinch. It was noisy with rooks flying into their rookery. The tups were being fed up into prime condition in readiness for their season of employment.

16 *September* 2006: *Bradleyfield Allotment*

A glorious day with wisps of high cloud in a blue sky and high temperatures. Near Bradleyfield Farm there is a pasture with clearance cairns and a scattering of tall thistles and the twittering of goldfinch caught my attention and beyond the sheltering dry stone wall they fluttered onto seed heads and set them swaying, their bodies curved to balance upon those spine-tipped bracts and all amongst the thistles there were gleams of golden wing bars and that domino six of black and white down their backs. Clusters of seed were pecked out, and dislodged thistledown drifted on the breeze. Something frighted them and the charm took off and came down again a little further off in more seeding thistles. Few had the adult red and black face mask , so there must have been many juveniles. Suddenly, the charm vanished into the dark foliage of a hawthorn which filled with their music, the tinkling of tiny bells.

17 *September* 2006

Next day was warm and hazy. The thistles had lost their charm and had an end-of-season look; weather-beaten, a contortion of spines and stems with the sap gone out of them, all browned off.

18 September 2006: Scout Scar

Swallows and a pair of ravens flew the escarpment. A kestrel came down in an ash. I flushed a couple of snipe from heather, the first I've found hereabouts.

21 September 2006: Durham Bridge Wood and Whitbarrow

Fruitful September: hazel nuts, long ropes of bryony berries, scarlet hips, blackberries and at our feet windfall apples and ripe damsons along the woodside track that approaches the Whitbarrow limestone grassland. Above the ridge to Hervey's Monument the air was thronged with swallows feeding in the hot sun. Hazy views toward Scout Scar: offsets of limestone cliff, grass buttress, scree slope and woodland. Damsons were being picked in the Lyth Valley orchards and we bought some from Dawson Fold, close to the Lyth Valley Arms. They are a speciality of the area and delicious.

Three scars. Foreground: gorse and heather on Scout Scar Escarpment. Centre: Barrowfield Farm pastures and the crags of wooded Burnbarrow Scar, with Helsington Pool down in the Lyth Valley to the right. Centre distance: White Scar and Whitbarrow. 29.4.2008

22 *September* 2006: *Scout Scar*

A cloudy afternoon on Scout Scar where swallows were mustering. They swept low along the escarpment edge but there was a change in behaviour: they gathered in trees up on the cliff top. There were several in the crown of a hawthorn and when I came close they did not fly. They were juveniles, without the glossy blue on their backs, without the red on forehead and throat. They must be from a late brood for one was still food-begging. Were they tough enough for the long haul flight to Africa? I was there to wish them God speed.

I love these seasonal shifts; relishing the last of the swallows for this year. Sitting half-hidden by a hawthorn, with my feet touching the cliff edge, I was caught up in the ellipse of swallow flight as they skimmed the cliff and rose above me, then swept down the escarpment and skimmed the canopy of the wood below. Now above, now below and all around, they wove me into their skein of flight. They flew dark against the dark crowns of the trees below with glints of white in their twisting flight and flew up the bright rock face with its slivers of dark yew and fruiting whitebeam, up over the cliff with their streamers etched against the sky. And above the canopy there was a gleam of constant white in the long, gliding flight of house martins with their white rump. Martins too were come to the muster. Hirundines everywhere.

26 *September* 2006

A kestrel carrying its kill came down in a hawthorn and picked at it. At noon, Scout Scar was in obscurity. To the south, a couple of figures were caught in silhouette on the horizon, the waters of the Kent estuary and Morecambe Bay were ablaze, and sunlight that fringed the clouds in brilliance illuminated a swathe of the Lyth Valley. The fells were sunlit and shadowed and someone on the divine lighting console took pleasure in ranging the spotlight over the landscape to His delectation. As I headed back north, sunlight was diffused over the Scar. There was the soft note of a bullfinch, a raven called and flew past and a pair of buzzards soared above the cliff as swallows swept by. Later, a pair of kestrels took their place. The male scanned the scree buttress scattered with slender ash, yew and whitebeam. He hung on the air, wings outstretched and feathers trembling in the wind, his tail fanned and each black-tipped feather distinct as he played the air currents along the cliff edge.

1 October 2006: Brigsteer Park

Returning from Leighton Moss, Irene and I stopped off at Brigsteer Park and made our way down, down past a tree laden with crab apples, past beech, oak, ash and coppiced hazel down beyond the last semblance of track through the last of the wooded limestone to reach the flat, peaty ground where the catchwater follows the western edge of the wood and Park Moss and the network of drainage ditches spreads over the Lyth Valley and the soft, silt bed of the catchwater was afloat with cress-like water plants and overhung with alder, its green fruit and its next spring's buds showing together.

In this trackless and secluded south-west corner of Brigsteer Park ancient coppice boles are scattered on soft, dark soils and dead wood litters the woodland floor. There are rotting trunks where mosses, ferns and pale green lichens grow. There is dampness, decay, and tiny pale fruit bodies of mosses. A heavy shower drenched us as we sought a way upward and back to the road. The scarlet berries of bittersweet and waxy red yew arils lay fallen on the ground beneath some splendid yew trees. Amongst dead nettles were the ghosts of bluebells, and the ghosts of a long-dead landowner and his deer park. In 1713 Walter Strickland of Sizergh was successful in petitioning to reroute a public way for *passengers* whom he hoped to keep clear of his deer, so he built a 'substantial' wall at Brigsteer Park and diverted the public way to the west side of it.

8 October 2006: Scout Scar

Grasshoppers were audible beneath a south-west wind on Scout Scar and through it came the call of stonechat and the cry of a buzzard which soared over Honeybee Wood and ravens flew dark against a blue sky along the escarpment edge. To the south, the sun gleamed off the waters of the Kent estuary and a hovering kestrel showed in silhouette, its feathers riffling in the wind which lifted and buoyed up the bird and the spirits on an exhilarating afternoon. And the dark silhouette of a butterfly arced across the hovering kestrel. A shadow swept above me and over the cliff edge as the kestrel rose on an updraught and hung hovering. Then in its downward sweep it was caught in light and full colour.

17 October 2006: Bradleyfield Allotment and Helsington Barrows

So warm, like the air above an over-heated swimming pool. On Scout Scar, there was a bluish sky directly above and sunlight struck the cliff-edge but fog obliterated the fells to the west. Whitbarrow was a soft outline merely, the Kent estuary was blotted out and toward the sea an ethereal, luminous fog filled the lower reaches of the Lyth Valley. I walked toward Helsington Barrows enthralled by the light that rendered the fog beautiful and evanescent. A south wind blew up suddenly and visibility improved but the magic was gone.

Picked up a kestrel as I approached Bradleyfield Farm. The light was poor and I wouldn't have located him had he not called and kept on calling.

22 October 2006: *hound trailing on Cunswick Fell* (*from letter to David*)

Remember that sunny afternoon in August, an orienteering rest day, when we went to Ings and sat on a grassy bank to watch Cumbrian wrestling, sheep dog trials and hound trailing? There was a loud speaker to tell spectators all about these local sports and we were asked to cheer the hounds home as they raced for the finish line and I did and you didn't, neither of us being much good at audience participation but here it felt right.

There is a Kendal hound trailing course and the venue is either the race course at Bradleyfield, or Cunswick Fell where they assembled today. Barbed wire along the route was lagged, the road was manned to alert drivers to hounds crossing, two men had set out to lay the trail, each covering half of the course and bearing a long swathe of rag soaked in aniseed and paraffin and a plastic bottle from which to keep it soaked. There was a ten-mile race for hounds, half the distance for puppies. There is betting on these races so bookies set up their stands and the names of the favourites were chalked up. Plenty of opportunities for hound trailing aficionados to make money. Yesterday there was hound trailing at Lorton, this coming week at Eskdale, Threlkeld and Sandale.

Competitors, each with a handful of caged hounds in the back of their vehicles, were arrived on the fell. Hounds were exercised and off to the start: lithe on taut leashes. They're athletes, I was reminded, and as a hound jumped up on its hind legs against its owner's body I could see how long, lean, narrow in the loins and finely muscled it was. Its clipped coat made its ribs visible. There was a palpable excitement and a yelping and yowling. Owners patted them, bent over them holding them between their knees in an image of bums and thrashing tails in those last, close, confiding moments. Then they were slipped and it was jackets off, leashes off and they were away, leaping over a wall and toward Bradleyfield you could hear them go. Soon we would be looking north, toward distant Kentmere Pike and Sleddale Fell and the cairn on Cunswick Fell where we would pick them up as they sped over the fell where Sunday lunchtime runners and walkers might suddenly see hounds bearing down on them and making for the same gate in the fence. And there was a yelling out of hounds' names to bring them home as they raced for the finish line and the second they crossed it a bowl of food was placed before them and they were back on the leash.

Respite. A pair of buzzards circled mewing over Cunswick Scar and a goldfinch sang in the top of a leafless ash. Two little lads played in the base of a hawthorn, and from within parked vehicles came the whining and occasional yelping of caged hounds awaiting their race and the smell redolent of the hound regime. Conversation was all about hounds past and present, of hound trailing venues and of owners. Men reminisced with nostalgia for 1972 and a winning hound called Romulus: 'Them were good hound trailing days then. Best days are long since gone.'

They were friendly and welcoming, the local hound trailing fraternity. The promoter, Russell Dawson, has five hounds at home. His father and grandfather followed the sport and he hopes his children will too. Hound names declare their blood lines and ownership. Town Crier is owned by the Kendal town crier, Mike Wilding. His wife Dorothy has a hound called Mossy Dora, in memory of her mother Dora Moss. Sparrowmire Hunter and her owners come from Sparrowmire Lane. After the race she was checked for injuries. None. A red antiseptic scrub was squirted on her back and water was sponged carefully all over her. Her claws were checked (they can split) and pads can blister on the sharp limestone. Hounds can cut themselves on barbed wire and if they race through a herd of cows they could be injured. For this hound, all was well.

23 October 2006: *Scout Scar and Helsington Barrows*

Mid-morning and there was a veil of rain moving east from the fells and the Langdales were all pellucid cloudlets and soft, magical outlines. Just a flank of mountain lit here and there, all else opacity and translucence. There was a curve of rainbow across the Lyth Valley and as I walked south it seemed to follow me, now arcing over Barrowfield Farm with its foot (and crock of gold) right in the slurry pit, now over Honeybee Wood, now in an arc entire that touched down upon Scout Scar. A sunglasses and waterproofs morning. The limestone on the path gleamed in the rain and sun and raindrops sparkled on hawthorn, and slanting rain came shot through with sunlight along the ascent to the larch track and the ruin on Helsington Barrows. Ravens were over Scout Scar in deep, gurgling voice. Whitebeam had red berries but the wind had stripped them of leaves. Fungi continued abundant and there were lush, scarlet hood in the grass descending from the Scar.

24 October 2006: *Scout Scar and* Helsington Barrows

From the Kendal bypass, I saw a pall of fog delineating the course of the River Kent, a sign of an autumn morning. A thin layer of fog overlay the green pastures down in the Lyth Valley and the sun would slowly burn it off. A blue sky with only the dispersing white trajectories of flight, carbon emissions marked across the sky. This time of year the woods about Barrowfield Farm are in shadow until the sun is due south and the pheasants sun themselves on the cliff top. The Capitoline geese of Barrowfield, they give a cackling alarm at an approaching runner and scuttle to the cliff edge and launch themselves in a heavy-bodied glide down into the sunlit pastures where they strut among the Swaledale sheep.

Walking south into the sun is dazzling, and today creates an enchanting play of darkness and light. By the cairn I glimpsed a gleaming wing, a fluttering lost in sombre hawthorn as the sun cast all into gloom and silhouette. A glint of dark wings transfixed with light: into-the-sun-obscurity but the effect was striking. I was seeing something wonderful and scarcely seeing it. The silhouette seemed to

Oyster mushroom on a Helsington Barrows sycamore.

show forked finch tails. Birds flitted about the bushes and down into the heather, caught the light, assumed that yellow edge on the primaries and resolved into greenfinch, never so transformed into magic.

On Helsington Barrows, I made for a larch grove with mature trees stately of form with sweeping boughs, some raised on a knoll so the light struck through their green-gold foliage in a contrast with yesterday's deep gloom. On a rough and off-piste exploration I eventually found myself at the almost leafless sycamore where the green woodpecker nested. The bark is scabbed into rosy tesserae and above the nest hole there was layer upon layer of cascading oyster mushroom of a creamy pink. The tree, ravaged by decay and the attentions of invertebrates and the green woodpecker, is rotten to the core and hollow at its base. Its branches die back yet it lives and gives nourishment to fungi and a nursery to a green woodpecker.

A flock of mistlethrush was vocal and feeding on yew berries and from the dark foliage came the flash of pale underwings. By midday it was hot once again. The sky was changing all the time and deep indigo clouds formed over the Langdales and over Morecambe Bay. Light rain before I reached home.

Sunday 29 October 2006: *hound trailing on Cunswick Fell* *(from letter to David)*

A beautiful day and below Cunswick Fell the trees of Scar Wood were metallic, autumnal shades with silver birch all golden leaved. Would the hounds cope with the swollen crossing of the beck down at Tranthwaite Hall? Well they all came racing down the home straight, all six of them, the challenge of the flooded beck without witness.

Amused that you mountain marathon runners faced a similar challenge during the incessant rain of Saturday when you and your mountain marathon partner, each man with 14 lbs of kit in a rucksack, swam across a remote Galloway beck in spate. Overwashed banks so you waded in feeling for the hidden drop and then swam the 10–15 metres of this dark and peaty beck. Like the hounds swimming unobserved, except that you revelled in the telling of the tale. What bravado, the swimming of Clough Lane, and what an unlikely name for a beck!

1 November 2006: *Scout Scar escarpment*

Now the woods below Scout Scar were looking fine with abundant golden birch and hazel a mellow yellow. Whitebeam had lost their leaves but their red berries gave colour and the bare, bright limbs of slender ash stood out against the autumnal foliage. The escarpment edge is exposed to the south-west winds so its trees are quickly stripped bare, although the yew is ever a sombre green.

Scout Scar escarpment has secret shelves and ledges that can only be glimpsed from the hints of paths close to the edge or if you venture onto the sloping buttresses. The limestone layers of the cliff are fractured into chunks with fissures and niches where whitebeam, ivy and yew can send out their roots. There are grassy platforms that cannot be seen from above. Hidden places. From early on this cold morning there had been a strong sun and the pheasants were up here taking advantage of it and they took off with a racket when I came too close. There's this covert life of the escarpment edge, close to the path but unseen by those who keep to it, their thoughts elsewhere.

Right to left: the limestone ridge with a thin scattering of hawthorn. The cliff terrace shows dark slivers of yew growing in the rock, then come buttress and scree slopes with wood descending to Barrowfield Farm pastures. 27.3.2008

Ash growing on limestone clitter with inset of breaking ash buds. 27.3.2008

9 November 2006: Bradleyfield Allotment and Helsington Barrows

A fine, sunny day with a little haze. To everything its time of splendour. The larch on Helsington Barrows were magnificent, sweeping up like candelabra, their needles a deep, golden green. Another still and quiet day. A jay squawked and fed in the leaf litter where the sycamore of the green woodpecker clings onto life in a wooded, south-facing dry valley that gathers light. Lucky I found the oyster mushroom when I did. Then it was fleshy and rosy-cream, now large chunks were fallen onto the ground and the rest had darkened and was shrunk.

The Bradleyfield tups would seem to have been busy and the ewes were red about the rump. 'Tupped up, tupped up, tupped up': thus Brian Bowness when telling me his ewes were in lamb.

11 November 2006: Cunswick Fell

Bound for Cunswick Fell on a morning of sunshine and showers after the strong winds and heavy rain during our walk in Kentmere yesterday. A foreground of winter trees gloriously sunlit with their crowns a delicate tracery against a bruised-looking sky. David and I walked up to the cairn on Cunswick Fell (which is the northernmost point of the limestone escarpment) then down through the gated stile into Scar Wood. A steepish, rocky path descends the wooded scarp slope which shelves out before the next shallow limestone terrace. Here springs emerge and a stream runs through the trees. It's a fine, mixed wood with coppiced hazel and wood piles as dead wood habitat. A footpath bisects the wood but it is the domain of pheasants. Limekilns are historic artefacts deemed worthy of protection and restoration and there's one toward Gamblesmire Lane at the foot of the escarpment, where scree might provide a supply of rock fragments.

13 November 2006: Bradleyfield Allotment and Scout Scar

Unsettled weather. The sun struggled to penetrate cloud and there was fleeting illumination of field or fellside, all else in gloom. Another day of rainbows, now over Cunswick Fell, now over Scout Scar. Veils of rain and shafts of sunlight through louring cloud. The south-west wind was strong and drowned out any sound in the landscape by buffeting my hood about my face and flapping my sleeves noisily. At the cairn above Barrowfield I turned east and went wandering over the bare, windswept landscape enjoying the way sunlight gleamed on the small, bare ash that grow on the abundant limestone clitter: ash trees which sometimes appear like slender figures in a dance. It's not unusual for an ash to divide, intertwine, and lean outward from a shared footing. Dancers in free space, ash with twin trunks spot-lit by strong sunlight. I sought out the Blue Stone, rough sculpture on its limestone plinth. Not so massive as the erratics of Kentmere but a landmark on which sunlight caught the weathered commemoration to the Chapman family.

30 November 2006: circuit from Cunswick Fell

Irene and I to Cunswick Fell where the grassy track had ring upon ring of large, brown fungi that we later found on Scout Scar too. Hawthorn yields to the prevailing wind and grows aslant, contorted, in barbed spines. And there are sculptures which might be yew or juniper, closely grazed to a height sheep might reach and then branching out into some semblance of their species. Like the Scout Scar escarpment, there is whitebeam and a band of yew growing on the steep scree. On lower ground are ash, coppiced hazel and oak. We went down through Scar Wood where the footpath comes close enough to Cunswick Tarn, with a noisy flock of water birds, to see that the tarn is surrounded by fen and some willow scrub. Via Cunswick Hall and Gamblesmire Lane to an encounter with frisky cows at Knott Hill. In the trees about Tullythwaite House there were redwing. Like fieldfare and mistlethrush, they overwinter in woodland with shelter and berries. The cliff of Scout Scar looked grey and even darker where yew grew on the face of the rock. Through Barrowfield Farm and up onto Scout Scar, exposed and inhospitable at this season. Windy and gloomy throughout the short day.

Tuesday 5 December 2006: *River Kent, through Kendal*

A prolonged spell of heavy rain, gale force winds and gloomy days. The River Kent raced by, all rocks submerged by the volume of water. Two smart male goosander, part of a small flock, kept close to the bank south of Miller Bridge.

Walking up Gillingate by moonlight I was surprised to hear the roaring of Blind Beck from beyond the houses and deep in the ravine. My friends who live here told me the issues in the ghyll were spectacular.

Friday 8 December 2006: *Scout Scar and Helsington Barrows*

A joy to see the sun upon the landscape amidst so many dark and stormy days. Predictably, the Lyth Valley was flooded. The mid-morning sun caught a few fieldfare and redwing in the fringe of trees south of Barrowfield Farm. More stormy weather gathered in the west and the skies over the fells were louring and dramatic. On my return walk north the sun was full on the woods which were at their most beautiful: contrasts of colour and form never finer. Deciduous trees showed subtle, hazy grey with birch crowns a deep purple whilst yew were solid blocks of green and not at all sombre in the strong light. It continues unseasonably mild but with nights of lashing wind and rain.

Fieldfare and redwing are the obvious winter visitors but the picture is more complex than might appear. With hard weather and a shortage of food supplies there can be an influx of chaffinch and wren from Scandinavia, starling from Russia, blackbird and robin from eastern Europe.

14 December 2006: River Kent, Kendal

None of my friends remembers such rain. On and on it goes. At Ghyllside, the issues spout forth in waterfalls and Blind Beck goes rushing down to the Kent, which is swollen and of a brown-olive colour and gone are its goosander and its dipper. It must have been exceptionally heavy rain in a concentrated time that triggered the flood of February 2004.

16 December 2006: Bradleyfield Allotment and Helsington Barrows

In the early hours of the morning tawny owls called to each other, the more distant bird so faint it was audible almost as an echo of the nearer owl. Possibly the bird that made an impression locally. I heard it smacked against a window and, when the bedroom curtains were drawn back, there was the image of an owl imprinted on the glass in perfect detail.

A fine day after all that rain, so said we all. In the trees about Bradleyfield catkins and scyamore buds were forming. Starlings perched in the crown of a tree until they were displaced by fieldfare. There was richly coloured Jew's ear fungus on elder, the tree on which legend declares Judas hanged himself, as Piers Plowman reminds the reader in Langland's fourteenth-century text. Strange choice, since elder is not a stout tree and the fungus appears on old elder with decaying limbs. Ear-shaped and fleshy, it is veined like an ear.

Snow on the tops, gleaming in the sunlight to the north and on Red Screes. A pair of buzzards circled close by St John's Church and a pair of ravens flew the edge, whiffling in the wind. The oyster mushroom on my drenched sycamore was now no more than a few gelatinous blobs, the ground littered with sodden chunks. The south-facing grassy slopes of Helsington Barrows are patterned with anthills, just where the sun can catch them. In winter the ants are less active but a warm, bright day will benefit the colony. There was a flock of gulls on the floodwaters of the Lyth Valley. In the strong sunlight winter heather glowed in muted colour.

22 December 2006: River Kent, Kendal

Fog prevailed. There was little water in Blind Beck and the Kent ran clear so the feet of the goosander showed salmon-pink and a bird scratched itself in a flurry of colour as the small flock swam close to the riverside walkway.

26 December 2006: *the Kendal Race Course*

St Stephen's Day and 400 years ago this day the first performance of *King Lear* was given at Whitehall before King James I.

There is a traditional charity Boxing Day hound trailing meet at the Kendal race course, Bradleyfield. A mizzling day, presided over with good cheer by the town crier. The puppies were in the slips, and off, sending staggering with a laugh the young woman who approached them laying the last of the trail. The town crier invited everyone to walk across the race course to the finish and as soon as the hounds appeared on the limestone scrub they were being hailed heartily home. He had asked owners to catch their hounds and they waited with a bowl of food in one hand and a leash in the other but the winner raced in and raced on, leaving his bowl of Christmas left-overs and sprinting over the race course with his owner giving chase. A race course is for racing. Why stop when you're ahead of the field and your blood is up? What's a finishing line to a puppy?

The scent of aniseed and paraffin lingers on the grass to tell of the hounds' presence. Visibility was poor, fog and murk had hung around for days. Scattered flowers showed on the gorse. The Kendal race course is marked on the map and still registered, although after 1947 it ceased to be used. The grassy circuit is still visible in the pasture and the rusting judges' stand lies toppled, an occasional perch for birds. The town crier had told me that the hounds would return toward the soot box which was the site of a former rubbish tip by a gate off the Brigsteer Road.

2007

10 January 2007: *Lyth Valley from Scout Scar*

The relentless gloom, wind and rain was oppressive. Today, respite. Along the escarpment edge the stony track and the grass gleamed in the rain. There came a rainbow as the sun struggled to break through, and triumphed. The fells had clarity, and some a topping of snow. The landscape opened up; there were horizons, possibilities. A mistlethrush was singing. With the Lyth Valley flooded it was easy to picture it as an inlet with the sheer cliff of White Scar looking out to sea and Whitbarrow above as a headland in dark and wooded profile. The flood waters defined it.

16 January 2007: *about Bradleyfield Farm – the in-bye land*

Calm before the storm. A flock of starling swept into the trees above Bradleyfield Farm. The bell-like tinkling of goldfinch came from the crown of an ash where the charm was busily feeding. Silent and still below them were birds which I could only make out slowly. Let there be light. The sun rose and slowly broke free of cloud and conferred upon the birds the colours for which they are named: *gold*finch and *red*wing. A robin sang, a raven called, there was the soft note of a bullfinch, greenfinch flew into the trees and disappeared and a wren hopped mouse-close over the mossy wall. The air was filled with birds calling; loudest, the volatile flock of starling that whooshed from the tree tops to come down in the open pasture of the highest field. Aggressive and vocal, a mistlethrush defended his larder of holly berries.

When I returned from Helsington Barrows hours later the sun shone full on fieldfare in the top of a hawthorn and blazoned their rich plumage as the starling whooshed about. In a shallow bowl low on the dip slope the pastures of the in-bye land offer the shelter of mature trees and are a favoured habitat. The intake wall is exclusive: it shuts out walkers and their dogs and so provides a haven for wildlife. Peer through the screen of shrubs and trees that line the field wall directly beyond the race course gate and it can be an entrée into a world of wildlife activity. This is the farmer's domain and long may it be so.

Today, the grass higher up toward the escarpment was stiff with frost and there was thin ice on puddles. There was another severe weather warning for Thursday and this sunlit calm with its unwonted activity was something rare.

17 January 2007: Bradleyfield Farm – the in-bye land

Tomorrow's severe weather was brewing. Redwing and goldfinch were faintly audible through the wind. Hidden behind the sheltering stone wall, Irene and I looked through a screen of shrubs for an intimate view of blackbird and redwing splashing and fluttering in a shallow rill and feeding with goldfinch down amidst the debris from the trees above. Tangled brambles, lichened hawthorn and swathes of ivy thick with dark berries would provide food and shelter for the stormy night to come. Follow the starling flock to find the fieldfare: that's what I've learned this winter. Sure enough, they were feeding together in a pasture. The sky darkened and a squall pelted us right across the race course but the landscape looked stunning in storm light.

19 January 2007: Bradleyfield Allotment and Helsington Barrows

Thirteen killed yesterday and hundreds injured in the UK in ferocious winds. Northern Europe took a similar battering. Up on the exposed escarpment the wind was still strong today.

By loudly defending his holly berries the mistlethrush pin-pointed the mixed flock in the pastures of the in-bye land that flew as dark starling with a glint of pale fieldfare plumage. In the crown of a sycamore, the starling chattered and the fieldfare were silent and discernible only by profile, discernible because I knew they were there. When the flock flew they separated out and the fieldfare made contact calls as they regrouped and flew off over Bradleyfield Allotment. I had pin-pointed their territory this winter and it wasn't the escarpment edge but these pastures and the wooded valleys of Helsington Barrows and its groves of yew trees with their fleshy red arils where fieldfare are often to be found high in larch and Scots pine.

These are my winter gleanings. This is all there has been for what seems a long, wild while. I've gleaned the light, the unrain, the lull in the storm.

23 January 2007: Lord's Lot

A bright day with snow on the tops and from Lord's Lot, west of Underbarrow, there were fine views east toward the Mushroom and the Scout Scar escarpment. At a height of 209 metres and over two kilometres distant the configuration of the cliff, scree and wood can be seen and the extent of the escarpment shows well. Orchards showed a few winter-withered damsons.

These sheltered pastures of the Bradleyfield Farm in-bye land have fringes of mature trees and shrubs that make it a favoured habitat for birds. 27.3.2008

27 January 2007: *below Scout Scar*

A day of brilliant light, with strong sun and shadow and unusual clarity on the fells. In the wood north of Barrowfield Farm there was pheasant shooting, with men snarling at dogs and beaters moving noisily through the winter trees invisible from the escarpment above. Pigeon flew up in alarm and a pheasant flew above the crown of the trees.

1 February 2007: *the River Kent*

Fog hung around all day with moisture in the air. Above Nether Bridge weir a dipper dipped over and over and disappeared to become a shimmer in the river, surfaced to shrug off a gloss of water and flew upstream to perch on a rock where its white throat pulsed with song, just audible above the Aynam Road traffic. I had been alerted to the playful pair of dipper by their call but I don't think I've ever heard one singing before. The flashing lights of an ambulance crossing Miller Bridge reflected on the river where a pair of mute swan swam.

3 February 2007: Bradleyfield Allotment and Helsington Barrows

Today began with clouds: altocumulus mackerel sky in intricate and changing patterns that lingered until midday, as did the heavy frost. Like yesterday, the glory of the day was in the sky and the Lyth Valley pastures had a misty pallor about them and moisture hung in the air.

Emerging from the trees in the central dry valley of Helsington Barrows, I heard a raucous jay, a green woodpecker and a flock of starling with fieldfare that flew calling and sunlit. The tree tops were full of fieldfare. The black Galloways grazed on the open limestone grassland, otherwise there was solitude, just the sound of birds in the trees and arrivals and departures.

By Bradleyfield Farm, a-squelch with mud, I fell into conversation with Tony Chapman, Brian Bowness, and their nutritionist who was there to change the feed since the sheep were not partial to the mix. Lambing is due to begin on 10th March and the ewes will be fed up in the weeks before. They explained how the different dyes on the ewes indicate which of them have mated during their cycle.

7 February 2007: Wells Garth and Brigsteer Park

Once again a cold, bright day with heavy frost. We crossed the race course, with mistlethrush, and made for Helsington Barrows where there were fieldfare in the trees of the dry valley. To St John's Church and through what was one of Sizergh Castle's deer parks where my friend Monica and I heard a drumming and found

Scarlet elf cup, Sarcoscyphaceae. Early in their season, these fungi show the perfect cup shape with white hairs on the outer surface. Scarlet elf cup has shown here on consecutive years.

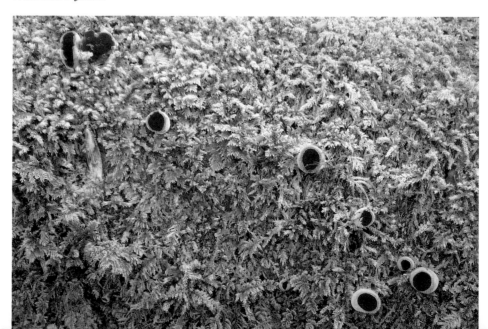

a great spotted woodpecker in an oak, watched it head-hammering and then its mate appeared. We crossed into Brigsteer Park where the ground crunched icy and coppiced hazel gleamed in the leafless winter wood. Heaped brashings form habitat for a variety of creatures. Decaying sycamore logs with bracket fungi were swathed in frozen moss with scarlet elf cup fungi, glossy red within the perfect chalice. So startling bright they looked like drops of blood against the whitened moss. We walked through the pastures to Park End Farm and up toward Wells Garth where springs issue from tree-clad rocks hung with icicles and a beck descends through waterfalls to the catchwater below Brigsteer Park and into the River Kent and its estuary.

Friday 9 February 2007: Scout Scar

A grey day with the ground hard-frozen and just enough snow to highlight footpath erosion and the pressure of walkers on this landscape. Broad highways converge on the major roundabout at the cairn which marks the track down to Barrowfield Farm. The farmer, Richard Gardner, has watched these paths grow significantly wider since he came here in 1966.

Snow reveals footpath erosion where a cairn indicates the track down the escarpment to Barrowfield Farm.

Sunday 11 February 2007

A warmer, misty day with the sun slow to appear, the ground thawed. There were goldfinch calling in a Ghyll Brow sycamore and snowdrops beneath it. Too steep for the plough, its pasture had been tilled by a creature whose signature was traced up the grassy bank in the form of molehills. Mounds of crumbly, freshly excavated earth have erupted on the race course too, as the solitary mole (not so solitary during spring mating) has tunnelled his way in search of slugs, earthworms, beetles, grubs, larvae and ants.

The yellow meadow ant, *Lasius flavus*, colonises Helsington Barrows and especially its south-facing, grassy slopes. Anthills are a striking feature of the landscape with a richer flora than the surrounding grass, as long as the colony is active and producing a fine tilth of soil.

Tuesday 13 February 2007: *the Lyth Valley*

Driving home across the Lyth Valley I put to flight a flock which included fieldfare so I backtracked, finding a cluster of veiny Jew's ear fungus on slashed elder in a hedge that once-upon-a-time had been carefully laid. There was the distant cry of a buzzard, the call of a raven and a mixed flock of field fare and starling foraged in the soft earth of a Lyth Valley pasture. From Helsington Pool Bridge I counted fifty teal. My walk took me along the outer fringe of the National Park, to Dobdale Hill – scarcely hill since the OS map shows a single contour ring amidst low-lying pastures which the raised and deeply ditched road cuts through, skirting Helsington Moss, tilting unpredictably and gently undulating over what would be wetland were it not for the pumping stations.

Sunday 18 February 2007: *Bradleyfield Allotment and Helsington Barrows*

A canopy of stars and frost at midnight.

In a clear sky a skylark sang, and I listened with my feet planted in thickly frosted grass. On and on it sang until I spied the bird shot through with sunlight above me. My first skylark of spring, they are returned to the upland of Scout Scar to breed.

On Helsington Barrows I spent a long while surrounded by fieldfare, a transient and wondrous while. They perched in the tops of larch trees thick with cones and I could make out redwing and starling amongst the numerous fieldfare. I was immersed within the experience, encircled with the flock, in the moment. Birds glinted in the sunlight as they flew high in the canopy. A woodpecker drummed close by and a great spotted flew, then a green woodpecker. A kestrel came down in a larch, his bright feet caught in the sunlight. Sunlight, solitude and bird song. Then the fieldfare were gone and the place was silent. The interlude was over. Back to the recitative after a fine aria.

Walking with my eyes focused on the crowns of the trees my foot slipped into a burrow and I saw the grass was riddled with them. The ageing sycamore are remarkable in form and in textures of exfoliating bark. There was a hole in a branch, too close to the ground to have nest potential so I probed it gently with an extended walking pole which disappeared, followed by my wrist, but at the thought of my arm being encased in a living branch I withdrew. Not ready for metamorphosis. Some of these old trees have hollow limbs, I discover. Often the natural sculptures of trees strike me as finer than most gallery exhibits.

National Trust parkland habitat with storm damaged Scots Pine and debris of its branches. 30.3.2008

This fallen bough of wild cherry has striking texture and patterns.

Sunday 25 February 2007: Bradleyfield Allotment and Helsington Barrows

Feeding time on Bradleyfield Allotment: the farmers scattered concentrates and sheep followed in their wake in a cacophony of bleating that drowned out the herald of the spring, the skylark. The pastures of the in-bye land have not been ploughed for some thirty years so this supplement is given to the sheep. Toward the height of the ridge, on fluttering wings and in full song higher and higher the bird ascended, taking me up and up into the air for the sublime interlude of its song until at last its wings were stilled, then closed as it plummeted silently into the grass so that when we both came down to earth I was disorientated. Where was I before the skylark sang?

This was an off-piste and erratic morning. The Blue Stone is the largest of the Bradleyfield Allotment erratics and I'm finding more of them on this rough and undulating ground. The smooth shape of a boulder and blotches of bright green lichen declare that it's not the local limestone.

In the stillness, the sound of church bells rose from the Lyth Valley to the escarpment edge.

What character they show, the senescent and storm-damaged trees of Helsington Barrows parkland! There are toppled oaks with limestone chunks gripped amongst their roots. Where its branches fork, a wild cherry has a gaping wound and resembles Munch's *The Scream,* the mouth's anguish. The bark of a fallen bough is smooth grey with a dark, rough-textured annular pattern crossed by frills of bracket fungi. A Scots pine lost great boughs in a winter storm a couple of years ago and there lay the decaying debris: a tangle of lichened twigs with pine cones, branches, and the boughs with plates and flakes of richly coloured bark riddled with beetle holes and with overlapping, greenish bracket fungi rippling along its bark which exuded a dark, gelatinous fungus, running into amorphous, watery blobs. Habitat galore within this debris. The tree lives on, with jagged and splintered stumps where two great boughs were wrenched off by torsion and the force of the storm: the power of destruction hinted at in the twisted fibres. Not a sign of rot, this is a thriving tree. For me, this Scots pine is a presence, renowned for interludes of fungi and goldcrest, an iconic tree.

So too is the majestic oak with the slit-in-the-bough where David had the fanciful notion of posting a letter. Amused by the recollection, I looked through the slit and there was shimmering daylight. Curving my arm under the bough, I raised my hand to the slit where my fingers appeared upside down: an inverted image. It must be the effect of a water droplet or a film of water acting as a lens. It felt like tree magic.

1 March 2007: St David's Day. Via Brigsteer and the Lyth Valley to Row

It's a rock and roll ride along the raised road to Row. Fifteen feet of rock had to settle for twelve months in the building of the road across the moss by Lord's Plain Farm, a Levens Hall tenancy. The farmhouse is built on oak piles. Before the draining of the mosses and the advent of reliable service roads there were corduroy roads. Some of these date back to the Bronze Age and are a criss-cross of branches of water-resistant juniper and of birch.

A day of faint sunlight with light rain and some snow on the tops. I walked beside the damson orchards, past the path junction where a wall abutting one of the lime kilns has collapsed. A stone wall encircles a place of bulrushes, and the wayside path was fresh with dog's mercury and cuckoo pint. There are fine views of Scout Scar from Row. This is the way to see the configuration of the escarpment; its cliffs, its scree slopes, its off-set terraces and a fault in the limestone that is exploited by the track up from Barrowfield. Burnbarrow Scar shows well from here.

I stopped in the Lyth Valley at Helsington Pool Bridge where the water was high after two days of rain. And fell into conversation with farmers from Tullythwaite Hall who pointed out the slabs of turf on the banks, the river having recently had its annual clean out as Helsington Pool receives water from the ditches and drains in the higher system. In the pasture beside the Pool were sheep with their lambs, two swans and oystercatchers. They have sheep and Holstein Friesian dairy cattle. We can have quality local milk from the lush, well-watered pastures of the Lyth Valley, no air miles and minimal road miles. What changes this landscape has seen: wetland to arable to sheep and dairy cattle, and the farmers know that some would like to see the valley return to wetland. 'After **our forefathers** dug out all the peat'; the farmer's phrase was telling, and personal. Working the Lyth Valley land is an inheritance, a continuity.

Here is continuity and an inheritance for me too. A morning spent like this is a reprise. Sometimes in the school holidays there were days out with my father, a valuation officer who met and befriended Yorkshire farmers in the course of his work, and we enjoyed being out in the countryside looking into a landscape and learning about it.

Tullythwaite Hall is in an Environmentally Sensitive Area and the farmers told me with pride of the conservation work being undertaken, and this includes fencing off some of the higher limestone knolls for the planting of hazel, birch and cherry.

2 March 2007: *Bradleyfield Allotment*

A song thrush sang in the same ash, on the same branch as last year's bird. Spring was in the air. Brian Bowness scattered concentrates for his sheep and hoped that each would find the quota allocated and would not trample it into the muddy thoroughfare churned up by the flock. He showed me the colour coding and the blue marks that indicate which ewes the scanner showed will bear twins, or triplets. The ewe about to lamb will find a spot, paw the ground, give birth and be taken indoors only for a 'clean up'.

Saturday 3 March 2007: *Bradleyfield Allotment and Helsington Barrows*

There was an intensity of colour and a depth of cloud moving fast in a stiff wind which suits kestrels and ravens revelling in the up-draught of the escarpment edge. I flushed a snipe and a hare. I found an owl pellet on an anthill: grey fur and tiny bones. Heather was rich in muted colour, a subtle mix of hues.

To Helsington Barrows where a fallen birch amidst bracken seemed to be scattered with dead leaves but it was fungi, with cryptic colouring. Last Sunday's Scots pine was a riot of fungi. There were greenish brackets running all along the branches and more of those deliquescing splodges the colour of dark treacle and even more gooey than before. And there was a fresh fungus extruding from beneath rosy-grey plates of dead bark, seethings of delicate pink. A thing of wonder, this dead and living tree. All beautiful, and strange.

Leafy brain fungus. There are bore holes made in the Scots pine bark by invertebrates.

No other Scots pine hereabouts showed Tremella and none showed in 2008.

Wednesday 7 March 2007: Bradleyfield Allotment and Helsington Barrows

A glorious morning; cold, fresh and bright. Spring quickens. Lark sing and curlew are back. I know where to look for hare; my second sighting of the week. I startled a green woodpecker into flight and heard them all morning, one close to my last summer's nest site. There had been no significant rain for 48 hours so I went to investigate my fine oak tree. Scar tissue has formed about the slit-in-the-bough and to see through it you have to be just in the right place and this time my fingers were pointing upward, as expected. So this branch of magic *is* caused by water acting as a lens. Yew trees bear yellow male flowers and were thick with them, and the first of the larch flowers were appearing. Juniper bear both their green and older black berries.

Lucky I studied the Scots pine fungi when I did because they were past their best. The treacle pudding was leafy brain fungus, *tremella foliacea*. Probably. The brackets were hairy curtain crust. The pink beauty may be a *tremella* too. I'm content that they were a great find. The mycologist friends I consulted had only my photographs to work on and that is not enough.

16 March 2007: Brigsteer Park

Dorothy Wordsworth's journal records their Gowbarrow Park daffodils on 15th April 1802. My own journal of 10th April 1993 notes when David and I found

Scarlet elf cup growing on dead wood, with dog's mercury.

them beside Ullswater. This year they have been in bloom for about a fortnight, so silk flowers have been planted at Windermere to guarantee daffodils at Easter! Thus regional news.

To Brigsteer Park where the flowers were perfect on a chilly, blustery day when winds would soon come in from the north and there would be snow. Drifts of delicate wild daffodils, dog's mercury, leaves of bluebells and the first primroses, all against a foil of leaf litter. The canopy is open and this is the season of the flowering and fruiting of the woodland floor: a time to rediscover my mossy log with scarlet elf cup in a startling explosion of colour, layers of luscious oyster mushroom, and abundant brackets. There was a shred of Jew's ear fungus too. Scarlet elf cup fruits on a lattice of mossy twigs and small branches strewn over the woodland floor and half-buried in dead leaves.

Sunday 18 March 2007: Bradleyfield Farm and Scout Scar

The sky grew dark and down came a pelting of hailstones that bounced off the window sill. Later in the morning, showers of snow and squalls of hail stung my face. In between, clarity and brightness. Powerful gusts on Scout Scar sent me reeling and my hood flapped furiously in a symphony of the winds. I avoided the more furious wintry squalls by sheltering with the lambs.

At Bradleyfield Farm lambing began on 10th March and, like last year, coincided with harsh weather. The race course field was saturated, the dew pond full and vehicle tracks about the farm made for churned-up mud. Brian Bowness drove in with a ewe and twin lambs just an hour old. He had brought three lambs off the race course, 'starved' with cold and with ice on their legs. The trio were in a pen beneath a heat lamp, their bodies shivery and trembling. Beside him was the farmer's survival kit: a selection of nourishment and anti-bacterial sprays. In extremis, he might inject glucose straight into a lamb's belly. It is vital that newborn lambs ingest the ewe's first secretion of colostrum which provides nutrition, energy and antibodies. He was watching a young ewe to ensure that she was making enough colostrum for her twins. Next comes true milk and a bellyful bulks out the tiny frame of newborn lambs. If they thrive their wrinkled bodies soon fill out: they grow into them. A ewe had lost her lamb, the farmer had skinned it and fitted this garment of white upon a black lamb whose face peered out from borrowed clothes. Confident that the ewe had accepted it as her own, he cut off the white skin and lifted the black lamb free. Tight-crinkled fleeces are muddy from the pasture, or stained ochre with afterbirth. When a ewe gives birth the umbilical cord breaks. A lamb with a long cord might tread on it, so the farmer cuts the cord and sprays the area with iodine to disinfect it: so tawny-bellied lambs with shrivelling umbilical cord. They gorge on milk and pump it out until they are clarted and clagged with it and the farmers wipe them clean of the yellowish mess. Tony Chapman was tending the animals, feeding protein cake and haylage to the ewes, changing their drinking water twice a day, gently lifting a dead lamb from a pen and checking all those unlucky to be born on such a harsh morning with Bradleyfield's first snow of the year. If harsh weather continued they would have to keep lambs off the fell for longer but would have difficulty accommodating them all and they are more prone to disease when penned up together. Orphan lambs are particularly vulnerable if colostrum is not given quickly.

In sheltered pastures close to the farm were lambs born during the previous week, looking sturdy and comparatively independent. They quickly take grass as well as ewe's milk. A ewe has only two teats and so giving birth to triplets challenges her capacity to supply enough milk. The battering winds struck the escarpment edge and this dip slope should be sheltered, although the farmers regretted the wide-open barn entrance on such a wild day.

19 March 2007: Wells Garth, Kist Wells and Brigsteer Park

A glorious morning with traces of snow on Helsington Barrows where David and I listened to fieldfare and starling silhouetted in the crowns of trees. From St John's Church we took the track down the wooded limestone escarpment where the cadence of waterfalls comes upon the ear, and at Wells Garth water issues from mossy rocks: a hymn to water, pure cascading spring water. All around was the sound of braided becks and in the gardens grew comfrey, scilla, primrose, varieties of miniature daffodil, and hellebore. The beck tumbles down through the pasture above Park End Farm, down by the orchard of apple and damson trees, across a pasture to the catchwater that runs below Brigsteer Park and out to the Kent and its estuary. David found a spring which rises in the wood below the church, carves a course across the pasture, then sinks into silt with a swirl and plops into crevices in the limestone to emerge below the farm as Sand Beck, soon to meet the catchwater. This is a water symphony, with beguiling silences as water sinks, vanishes and resurfaces in whimsical fashion. With beautiful spring water from a beck that never dries who needs mains water? In the mid-twentieth-century Park End Farm was required to install mains water for dairy cattle. Even in the summer of 2006 there was a trickle of water here in this beck.

Ewes and lambs feed in a
pasture with clearance cairns.
There is rough grazing on the
exposed ridge beyond, with
limestone clitter, juniper and
hawthorn.

The signature of a limestone
landscape: its dry-stone
walls. Clusters of hawthorn
in a shallow bowl on the dip
slope add to the shelter these
pastures of the Bradleyfield
in-bye land afford for ewes
and their lambs.

The farm is situated on limestone, just above the catchwater, where it meets the mosses. Until the 1830s it would have been on the edge of wetland. Even in the 1930s the farmers at Park End were putting a lot of effort into improving the drainage. They cleaned out dykes every year or two. Their farm has OS maps showing all the land drains or field drains. Its pastures abut Brigsteer Park where the daffodils were delicate and fresh, the mosses thick and bright, although the fungi on the mossy log seemed blighted by the wild weather.

Fine light along the escarpment edge. Blustery, but nothing like yesterday's wind.

On Tuesday and Wednesday we had splendid winter walks with snow and ice in the Langdales and on Place Fell.

Saturday 24 March 2007: Bradleyfield Allotment and Helsington Barrows

Three new lambs born at Bradleyfield and a glorious morning of sun and bright blue sky. With the exuberance of new legs freed from the confines of the uterus, they soon go frisking after Brian Bowness in a way that delights him: auditioning for a star role in *Billy Elliot*. For purposes of traceability, lambs are given double sided ear-tags within 24 hours of birth. On one side, the specific number accorded to the lamb. On the other, the holding number which identifies the farm where it was born. Colour coding gives the farmer the year of birth. Tail rings are affixed because longer tails attract blow flies and maggots. The lambs are castrated. At this farm they buy in tups so that they are unrelated to the ewes and provide a different blood-line. All movement of stock is required to be noted in the farmer's stock book.

A flock of over twenty curlew was caught in the light, in lilting, bubbling call. A skylark soared with a song to counter the curlew. A hare jinked away into a covering of hawthorn. Amongst the grass, hawthorn stumps showed where last spring the farmers opened up the land for their sheep, working with Natural England to promote flora.

Above Burnbarrow Scar there is a *cheval de frise* of stunted, heavily grazed blackthorn suckers set to trip and stab if one approaches the taller shrubs beside the dry stone wall where honey coloured insects nuzzled into a burst of fresh, white flowers with yellow stamens. The blackthorn has long, lancing spines and its latin name, *prunus spinosa*, acknowledges their quality. Blackthorn is a mass of pink buds and flowers before its leaf buds open. It is one of the first flowers of spring.

My route of the day went below the escarpment which has wet flushes amongst birch, alder, ash and hazel that border the Barrowfield pastures. Ash and yew are rooted below the cliff in chunks of scree. In the home pastures were their new lambs. Up on the edge a kestrel hunted and two children built the outline of a house from limestone clitter.

31 *March* 2007: *Bradleyfield Allotment and Helsington Barrows*

No longer a race course with gravid ewes but with the burgeoning of the flock the pastures of the in-bye land had ewes with their lambs: lambs filling out in the warm weather of the last week, troops of lambs cavorting and capering. Brian Bowness zipped about on his quad bike feeding his flock and they went bleating to meet him.

Pipit were returned to the Scar and willow warbler and, closer to home, chiffchaff. Exploring on the Helsington dip slope, I came across a stretch of limestone pavement with a perfectly sculpted pot with a spiralling inner ring, a few clints and grykes and *mille feuille* chunks of limestone, all this amidst rafts of clitter. The flower heads of blue moor grass look dark until one stoops to look closely at their delicate, steely-blue flowers. Up here on Helsington Barrows grazing comes courtesy of the Welsh Blacks and Galloways, the management tool employed by farmers in pursuit of Natural England conservation objectives. Not all cattle could thrive on a diet of bents and blue moor grass but Welsh Blacks and Galloways convert it into beef. Their hooves have a knocking effect on tufts of old dead grass. Cattle break up bracken litter, found on soils of some 6-inch depth, to encourage violets and primroses which are the food plants of the fritillary butterfly. Their grazing creates space for different herbs and promotes diversity of flora. Blue moor grass is rare nationally but here it can grow rank and tussocky and tends to dominate. The aim is to achieve a delicate balance: blue moor grass with other herbs.

View of Scout Scar escarpment from Barrowfield
Farm. The image shows a nursery pasture for their
Swaledale lambs and ewes. 2.5.2008

Barrowfield Swaledale ewes and lambs graze on Scout Scar during spring and summer.

Wednesday 4 April 2007: Bradleyfield Allotment and Helsington Barrows

A warm and sunny morning with clear skies. A male kestrel perched beside the nest niche of 2005 and 2006. Wheatear were returned to their breeding site. Skylark sang over the open scrub. Two dead rabbits in the grass: one decapitated, the other gralloched. The trees were taking on an aura of green. Sticky chestnut buds were opening.

Blackthorn is abundant but often it is grazed hard, ground hugging and overlooked. Ancient and enduring scraps grow on the limestone clitter. Anyone looking for classic limestone pavement would not come to Scout Scar but there are fragments with water-eroded features and flora that exploit the sheltering grikes and pot holes where nutrients are scarce. Thick knots of gnarled, grey blackthorn lock down into a grike and younger spines reach out over the rock like a cluster of glossy spiders, each with long red legs splayed out in the sun which cast shadow-spiders on the limestone. And beneath its flowers was an exquisite rue leaved saxifrage with red leaves and the tiniest white flower.

Blue moor grass flowering above Scout Scar. The network of open joints in the carboniferous limestone makes the rock fast draining.

Good Friday 6 April 2007: Bradleyfield Allotment

The female kestrel has joined her mate and they look set to breed, as do the wheatear. An Easter hare loped away before me. The delicate flowers of blue moor grass were tipped with pollen and the first violets appeared. Curlew flew overhead calling and small birds were singing in the hollies and hawthorn. The rafts of limestone clitter had a desolate look, strewn with twists of wizened blackthorn, black as if fire-scorched and frazzled. But there were a few perfect spine-stems close to the rock and bearing delicate flowers now fully open and with red stamens against white petals. Variation on a theme of blackthorn.

Saturday 7 April 2007: Bradleyfield Allotment

A warm afternoon to linger about the limestone. Curlew went up in bubbling voice. A lark chirruped and flew up into a hawthorn as I encroached upon his place. A hare loped away but a movement above the dead bracken gave it away and it came to rest and sat quite still, ears erect, a flush of warm brown on its nape. The saxifrage blooms apace on these warm, dry days, flower stems now rising proud from the rosette of succulent leaves with glistening white hairs. Two of the plants grow at the base of a runnel with herb robert in a thick cushion of moss which will collect water when next it rains. Obtaining water in this limestone landscape must be a challenge for flora and fauna. It takes several visits to begin to understand the ecology of this micro-habitat.

The more one walks this landscape the more erratics appear. They're not always significant boulders. There are aliens in the dry stone walls and a flush of colour makes them stand out. Amidst the jagged-edged slats of limestone there's the occasional warm-coloured cannon ball of rock with ochre and green lichens. The grey-white lichens on limestone merge into the intrinsic colour of the rock. Lichens encrust the Blue Stone, obliterating the sculpting of the Chapman dedication with shades of green, dried out, ancient lichens.

Blackthorn flowers on limestone with white lichens.

Fragment of limestone pavement with blackthorn locked down into the sheltering grikes. Inset: detail showing the thick stem of a dwarf but aged plant.

Sunday 8 April 2007: *Bradleyfield Allotment and Helsington Barrows*

Bright sun but today with a wind to keep the temperature a little lower. Where the track descends to Barrowfield Farm the silver birch were a haze of fresh green, the colour of its bursting leaf buds and greenish catkins. On Helsington Barrows a male great spotted woodpecker was drumming loudly in a chestnut whose leaf buds were beginning to open. Nearby, a green woodpecker was calling. Relaxation in the sun for the lambs of Bradleyfield Farm.

14 April 2007: *Bradleyfield Allotment and Helsington Barrows*

An unseasonably hot and humid, enervating day. Haze took out the views. Warm weather and lack of rain over the last few weeks was apparent and the race course ground crunched underfoot. The swallows returned two days ago. A kestrel flew into its nest niche and the male wheatear, with golden throat and looking very smart, stood sentinel. There were some thirteen ewes yet to lamb. Two had been lost to the fox and carrion crow pecked the eyes and tongue from two living lambs, to the farmer's disgust.

A stonechat was singing and offered what appeared to be a display flight and a willow warbler reclaimed his territory. This was the season of violets and a bedding of moss suits them well. Blackthorn was buzzing with pollinating insects and some of the flowers were already faded. The song of the nuthatch rose from the wood below the escarpment to meet the song of larks and pipits up on the ridge. As I was picking my way over limestone clitter warmed by the sun a lizard shot away before me. With no rain the rue leaved saxifrage must depend on overnight dew that moistens the moss in which it grows.

Monday 16 April 2007: *Bradleyfield Allotment*

Still no rain and cracks appeared in the earth where the race course field leads onto the open fellside. There was haze but Whitbarrow was visible and there was some definition in the skyscape: fine mackerel sky with some Cumulus cloud. Warm but not oppressive. A skylark, crest erect, sang on the top of a hawthorn. The woods were greening and I had never seen so many violets in the grass on the escarpment. And bumble bees were abroad. My handsome wheatear sang on his rocks. A flock of black back gulls called over the race course.

Wednesday 18 April 2007: *Helsington Barrows, Barrowfield Farm*

Today, there was defined Cumulus against bright blue and the fells distinguished themselves in unusual clarity. The air was fresh but still no sign of rain. The male wheatear sang on his sentinel stones – it's the time of year for breeding birds to be in full song. Beneath the trees on Helsington Barrows there were violets and wood sorrel. Strawberry plants were flowering.

Remembering the bluebell leaves in the wet flush of wood below the escarpment, I returned on the path below. It's a discrete habitat, quite unlike the characteristic limestone upland. Fenced off and undisturbed by man or dogs, it thrives on the non-intervention approach. There is a streamlet flows through it, something of a pond, ramson leaves, wood anemones, primroses and bluebells and coppiced hazel. There was another dead rabbit, an outbreak of myxomatosis. On the path ascending from Barrowfield was an early purple orchid and whitebeam was breaking into tulip-like buds. The first swallows arrived at Barrowfield Farm two days ago. Close by the farmhouse there is an orchard of damson trees whose flowers were already past their best. Sunlight picked out Burnbarrow Scar and the wood below with its delicate fresh foliage. In the pastures there were ewes with lambs and pheasants. I had a long chat with Barbara Gardner, the farmer's wife, who told me of a morning during the Foot and Mouth epidemic when six deer stood on the escarpment edge outlined against the sky. Within those months when access was barred wildlife reclaimed the place. They had a rigorous disinfecting drill regarding the arrival of the tanker which comes every other day to collect milk that is stored in a refrigerated milk tank. The tanker driver checks that it is the correct temperature before pumping it into the milk tanker. Their dairy cattle are black and white Holsteins. Up above the escarpment their Welsh Black cattle were grazing: the flora management tool. Not a hint of April showers but the May flowers were already here. Spring is come early and, with hot sun and no rain, it comes in a rush and will be over all too swiftly.

21 April 2007: *Bradleyfield Allotment with geologist Colin Rowley*

Typical April weather, cool and slightly hazy. My first cuckoo of spring sang somewhere on Bradleyfield Allotment, a willow warbler sang in the top of a holly and his kin sang everywhere.

We were come on an erratic foray. It's possible to pick out the Blue Stone from the Brigsteer Road, just below the skyline. It is pyroclastic rock from the

Erratic on limestone bedrock; this one is known locally as the Blue Stone.

Borrowdale Volcanics Group. Volcanic breccia spewed into the air and came down not far from the volcano that produced it, probably within fifteen miles from here. Its fragments are angular, a chaotic jumble of bits of different sizes. It has a layered structure and the planes within it are caused by a succession of explosions and eruptions within the same episode. There's a nearby boulder of comparable geological composition. The erratic, which reminds me of a table top, is a very fine grained volcanic ash. On one side it has lichen Colin dubs pistachio colour. There are fragments of friable sandstone in the grass around it. There is diversity in these glacier-dumped older rocks on the base limestone and once you begin to search you see the different sculpting of the rock and colourful lichens which do not grow on alkaline limestone. The dry stone walls, built of material collected from the fields, include smaller rounded lumps of rock dumped by the glacier which carried on dumping boulders and debris on its course across what is now Helsington Barrows.

This scattering of erratics is to be found on the Scout Scar dip slope, half-concealed within a stronghold of native juniper and something at the heart of a bush caught my eye. We kept searching and found more and more of the stuff. A profusion of fungus, orange and jelly-like or dark and shrivelled, erupted from juniper bark. I had never seen such an outbreak and wondered had I missed it in previous years or was this unprecedented?

22 April 2007: *Bradleyfield Allotment*

It had rained during the night and continued to rain all day. Irene asked if I would show her the rue leaved saxifrage and the mist was so heavy on higher ground that it was disorientating, even though I had frequently been here in this spot of late. Landmarks were gone and the Blue Stone loomed out of the mist only when we came close to it. In poor light, the fragment of limestone pavement and its saxifrage looked forlorn. But the juniper fungus was spectacular. The rain had re-hydrated it and the slightest touch to a juniper bush set the jelly filaments quivering and every bush seemed festooned with gaudy orange flowers, like pom-pom chrysanthemum. I went home for my camera and secured a few shots, which was fortunate because next day the fungus was utterly unremarkable. Days of rain appeared to have leached the colour out of it. Two weeks later I could find no trace of it. The fungus is one of the *calocera*, but which? Will it reappear in 2008 to give me a second chance?

Calocera *fungus growing out of a berried branch of juniper.*

National Trust parkland habitat with oak tree and anthills.

26 April 2007: *Helsington Barrows with Brian Fereday, National Trust Forester Warden.*

Head south from the Mushroom Shelter and the path above the Scout Scar escarpment follows the limestone ridge through open scrub with a scattering of small ash trees, juniper and hawthorn. Pass the wall, with trig point at 229 metres, where you leave the National Park and Bradleyfield and enter the parish of Helsington. This is part of the Levens Allotment, grazed by the Swaledale sheep and hardy Welsh Black cattle of Barrowfield Farm, which is a tenant farm owned by Levens Hall. You are now on Helsington Barrows. Continue walking south and above Burnbarrow Scar there is a wall with a gate that gives access to National Trust land. Within this enclosure there is a different look and feel to the landscape although topographically it is a continuation of the limestone ridge. Brian Fereday has managed this part of Helsington Barrows all his working life and I was meeting him out here to learn why the landscape looks as it does.

The wall was probably built about the time of enclosures, after 1815, when this area formed part of the Sizergh estate. The Stricklands of Sizergh planted it as an experiment, primarily with larch, between 1895 and 1900, thinning the plantation in the 1930s and clearing it for timber during the war, *circa* 1942. So we are seeing the remnants of the 1895 plantation. The Sizergh land was acquired by the National Trust in 1950 and the landscape now resembles parkland where you might expect to see deer; roe deer. Galloway cattle from the Cinderbarrow National Trust farm are here to promote the flora of this limestone grassland. The cattle-grazing regime followed by Cinderbarrow and Barrowfield evolved in discussion with Natural England and agricultural tenancies here are working in harmony with conservation objectives. Helsington Barrows is a Site of Special Scientific Interest and the active support and involvement of farmers is crucial. The National Trust land is contiguous with the Levens Allotment but the wall delineates a history of different ownership and different management in this 250 acres.

The north- to north-east zone is the most densely wooded, with groves of yew that attract fieldfare, redwing and mistlethrush and these native trees are intermixed with mature larch, Scots pine and deciduous trees that afford the perfect habitat for nuthatch, treecreeper, great spotted and green woodpecker. The ridges of the central area are intersected by dry valleys where clusters of oak and horse chestnut are planted. The higher ground rises to just over 200 metres and on the knolls there are distinctive stands of Scots pine and larch. There are mature trees, ancient trees of character and of sculptural beauty, dying, dead and fallen trees; like the wild cherry and my Scots pine which lost a bough in the winter storms of 2004 and stands surrounded by a debris of its own fallen limbs, supporting diverse fungi whose mycelia cause the decomposition of its wood to create habitat for invertebrates and their larvae. There are holes bored into the scales of its bark. Woodpeckers and nuthatch depend for their survival on this dead wood habitat. There are those who would wish to see dead wood tidied away but its presence makes a significant contribution to biodiversity on Helsington Barrows. These dead wood communities are important both here and in Brigsteer Park which Brian also manages.

This was a morning of exceptional clarity, with bright Cumulus and strong sunlight. Trees were flowering; the major oak with the slit-in-the-bough was resplendent with yellow male catkins and the freshest new foliage. It's close to the boundary wall so looking across toward the Coniston fells you can see the contrasting terrain of open scrub beyond. Recent rain had left the landscape lush and verdant. It was a warm, fragrant morning and from the Scots pine came elusive wafts of resin carried on the lightest breeze. Butterflies were abroad: speckled wood, orange tip and brimstone. The first flush of spring flowers appeared, with cowslip and early purple orchid. Throughout spring and summer the flora of Helsington Barrows is a joy.

Grazing patterns have changed and this is benefiting both trees and flowers. Some six years ago sheep were taken off the land and after the 2001 Foot and Mouth epidemic a herd of eighteen hardy Galloway cattle was introduced to encourage flora: they scuff the ground and create pockets where flowers will germinate. In grazing, they remove coarse grasses that sheep would not eat and so leave room for a greater diversity of plants. The finely worked soil of anthills supports exquisite flora and it is ironic that the Galloways sometimes head-butt them and bulldoze them flat. Circumstantial evidence is there at the scene of the crime in the form of fresh cow dung, and nothing else has the power to pulverize them. Fortunately, the ant colonies of this National Trust area are prolific and their serried ranks are to be found on the south-facing slopes, ants being responsive to heat. Green woodpeckers are partial to ants and their grubs and in August Brian has watched starlings and gulls gorging on flying ants. Anthills, I learn, are an indicator of unimproved pasture and could be up to 250 years old. It is the active ones which support the best flora and when the colony fails they revert to grass.

The Trust is trying to regenerate juniper which is a native plant particular to certain limestone soils and they attempted to pen plants about the edges so seed would fall and germinate within the fence, without success. When the sheep went the larch regenerated. Rather too well. Last September they had a *'staff pulling day'* to remove young larch which shade out other plants and whose needles acidify the soil; Brian showed me the border beyond the dry valley where they stopped and we saw stumps with strands of larch reappearing: it's persistent. There is tree planting, with young trees protected in wire. There are Caledonian Scots pine, their seed from Scotland but bought as young plants. Galloways reach into the penned Scots pine and tear at them and one of them has ripped off its ear tag in doing so. It must be rewarding for Brian Fereday to watch these penned Scots pine develop, having gathered some of them from the sandy shore of Loch Rannoch, grown them on in his garden, then replanted them here. Others have come from Foulshaw Moss.

He pointed out the conifers where crossbill were to be found several years ago. This I've heard before and I met someone up here who has them on video. Not all oral history is so easily authenticated and perhaps uncertainty makes it the more intriguing. There is a gate opposite High Wood on the Brigsteer Road which gives access onto Helsington Barrows and in the trees there are some half dozen feeders, always crammed with peanuts and seeds. Brian told me that some thirty years ago a Brigsteer man began to feed the birds and when he died it was carried on. The last find of the morning (and I'm not sure I could find it again) was shown to him some years ago by an elderly local man. Perhaps it was a managed rabbit warren. There are shallow entrances into covered limestone runs which might be natural features exploited by warreners, or might have been dug out. In medieval times managed rabbit warrens were a status symbol and this might have been a source of fresh meat and rabbit fur for the denizens of Sizergh Castle.

Herb paris, Paris quadrifolia. The plant has a solitary flower and five leaves is not unusual. Often an indicator of ancient woodland, herb paris occurs on calcareous soils, here and in the woods on Whitbarrow.

28 April 2007: *Warriner's Wood and Brigsteer Park*

A fine and sunny day for a bluebell walk. Warriner's Wood lies on the eastern side of the Brigsteer Road and abuts Helsington Barrows. It is ancient semi-natural woodland, under the aegis of the Woodland Trust. Its beech trees were just coming into leaf and the sharp green of fresh foliage contrasted with the bluebell flowers, leaf litter, beech mast and hazelnut shells. Sunlight touched the spathe of an arum lily to render it translucent with a delicate border of purple and the insect trap of its pitcher swollen green. Along the line of an old wall we came upon a patch of herb paris with a single plant in flower.

From here, we took a roundabout course through a landscape with swallows flying low over pastures and through fields of ewes with their lambs, to Sizergh Castle, across one of its former deer parks and out through high, deer-proof gates into Brigsteer Park. The woodland floor had dense swathes of fragrant bluebells sprinkled with wood anemone. There was a hum of insects with peacock and orange-tip butterflies over the flowers. I followed the flight of a butterfly that alighted as green-veined white, alighted on a yellow-green starry flower of the herb paris we had been seeking. A perfect patch of flowers amongst bluebell, bugle, wood anemone and dog's mercury.

Embayments are kept clear for butterflies: the silver-washed fritillary, the dark green fritillary, the brimstone, the hair-streak and the speckled wood. Areas beside the footpath are open to sunlight and that is just where our green-veined white appeared.

30 April 2007: *Durham Bridge Wood, Lyth Valley*

Irene and I spent a couple of hours in Durham Bridge Wood, just north of Row in the Lyth Valley. There were bluebells and a magnificent beech tree with the softest, bright green foliage, and grand oaks with acorns in the leaf litter, and cuckoo pint. A slender oak, newly coming into leaf, was plagued with the swollen, rosy-green galls known as oak apples. The gall wasp, *Biorhiza pallida*, injects its egg into the leaf bud which swells to form this structure around the larva.

1 May 2007: *return to Durham Bridge Wood*

Bluebells are an indicator of ancient woodland. A walk in bluebell woods is an English tradition and I love to discover where the best bluebells are. As a site of Special Scientific Interest, Durham Bridge Wood has undergone a rigorous survey and the results are available on the internet where I found we had missed its specialities. Irene suggested we might go again, so we did.

May Day was glorious. Beside the path approaching the wood there was a morel fungus, the first I've found in Cumbria. Within the wood, by good fortune, we met with Kath Jones walking her dogs and she took us about her wood to show us both *Daphne mezereum*, that we had hoped to discover, and spurge laurel *Daphne laureola*. Her bluebells with fragrant lily of the valley were something special.

We walked through a recently coppiced glade and found fresh bilberry leaves and flowers and water avens. There are log piles and dead wood habitat to encourage the biodiversity of the wood. Ten years ago, when living in Boxwood

Lily of the valley, Convallaria majalis, *growing with bluebells*, Scilla non-scripta.

Cottage, Kath used to watch playful red squirrels about the Scots pine as she was doing her ironing. These trees she nurtures in the hope the squirrels will return. She told us of an encounter with a man in a wet suit who was looking for the entrance to a cave he hoped to explore, and she spoke of springs emerging to form a stream that is diverted under the road by the Lyth Valley Arms. Someone carried out charcoal burning here until ten years ago. A lady moved out of her house and went back, a family with children being now in residence, because she had forgotten her arsenic!

3 May 2007: *Helsington Barrows, Scout Scar*

Another hot day with a cloudless sky and occasionally a hint of redeeming breeze. There are always fresh discoveries to be made. Today, a scattering of bluebells in bracken on the Barrows. The Scots pine were subtly and elusively fragrant and there were cowslip and violet in the grass close by and a coal tit fed in their branches. Wood sorrel flowered beneath larch trees. A cuckoo called three times as it flew from tree to tree, unseen.

On Scout Scar escarpment whitebeam were freshly coming into leaf. This is the season for the flowering of the cliff face, with the textured rocks yellow with hoary rock rose and common rock rose, the flowers of blue moor grass outlined against the blue sky and a mass of early purple orchid close to the cliff edge. Visible to anyone who pries into the twists and turns along the sinuous line of the escarpment, there is a secret rock garden: a contrast between the lavish flora of the cliff face and edge and the trodden path which is bare of flowers. Above Barrowfield Farm, a raven called and a crow closed his wings and dived at him, again and again. A male stonechat with a beak full of insects strutted a wall. The breeding wheatears sat beside each other on their rocks and if I approached slowly they seem quite comfortable with that, not being timid birds.

4 May 2007: *Scout Scar*

A sunny, fresh day with linnet. The Ghyll Brow meadow saxifrage pasture was beginning to bloom.

9 May 2007: *Along Scout Scar escarpment*

Depths of Cumulus cloud both brilliant and louring, light was fitful and rain was in the air, an inspiring sky. Swallows were feeding low and they swept up and about the escarpment edge. Song thrush, mistle thrush, curlew, willow warbler and skylark were singing and the soundscape drew me in, attuning me to the familiar, until a fresh song brought me to a halt where a beech tree rises up the face of the escarpment. The same song came from the top of a hawthorn and amidst the blossoms was a male redstart. In a holly was a third male in his best breeding plumage; grey back and rusty red from rump to tail and his black face turned toward me although he sang on seemingly unconcerned. Along the escarpment edge I had fine views of redstart upon redstart in full song. What a morning! They must be newly arrived from Africa.

How fresh and green the month of May! Honeybee Wood was a radiant green and high on the buttress of the escarpment the evergreen yew gave a dark contrast to the pale foliage of whitebeam, and hawthorn blossom. Grasses and flowering sedges upon the limestone ridge took on a hint of green. Along the cliff edge bird's foot trefoil flowered with rock rose, tormentil and a few white male flowerheads of mountain everlasting, cat's paw, *Antennaria dioica*. I was on my knees amongst cliff top flowers when I was struck afresh by the beauty of the season, of the day and of the landscape: the cool, rain-bearing skies and the brightness of the May wood caught in sunlight, the vista of the fells and this wondrous visitation of redstart. An epiphany; it was there all the time and today I saw it anew. Enlightenment. For me, there come to be landmark trees, trees I've been lost in: the swallow-mustering yew, the redstart holly and the fruitful whitebeam that grow about the rock face.

10 May 2007: *Scout Scar*

How well had I learnt redstart song? I went back to discover. The wind was strong and only the most determined songsters could be heard. The bracken was weather-beaten and flattened and the first new croziers emerged. Rain clouds over the fells came inexorably closer until the Lyth Valley was engulfed in rain which followed me home.

31 May 2007: *Scout Scar*

A fresh morning with starling feeding their dun-coloured fledglings in grass wet from yesterday's rain. I set out at 7.30 am and the rain clouds dispersed and the day became bright and warm. The kestrels flew from their nest niche and hunted low over Bradleyfield Allotment.

Deep within the foliage of beech and flowering whitebeam that rose from Scout Scar escarpment the redstart was singing. Spilling down over the cliff was common rock rose and hoary rockrose with its small, pale yellow flowers which open up only when the sun is strong on them. Hoary because its leaves are greyish. Here and at Humphrey Head this local speciality is at its northern limit.

Hoary Rockrose, Helianthemum canum, *growing on Scout Scar Escarpment.*

From Barrowfield, a bleating arose from the ewes and lambs penned in between two farmyard gates. The Lyth Valley fields were a patchwork of green and gold and some had been cut for silage.

Friday 1 June 2007: *Bradleyfield Allotment and Helsington Barrows*

It was warm and humid but gradually Cumulus became defined and a fresh breeze made for a perfect morning. You never know where the action will be and today it began directly, in the vicinity of Bradleyfield Farm where swallows were feeding. A cuckoo was calling from the open scrub beyond the race course and swifts circled above. A curlew called, a family of linnets flitted about the juniper and a pipit had a beak full of food.

From within the escarpment beech tree the redstart song appeared to bounce off the rocks. But if one ventured too close to the sheer cliff who knows how many fathoms down one might fall. The allure and mystery of cliffs! Last week, David scrambled cliff ledges in Gower seeking a frisson of danger and the perch vertiginous. There was samphire growing on the limestone and a sheer drop with waves pounding the rocks below and, 'lest deficient sight topple me down headlong', I chose a diversion where steep grass and a rocky pitch with scarlet pimpernel was thrill enough. The next evening we saw Sir Ian McKellen as Lear at the Courtyard Theatre, Stratford. With the power of *Lear* fresh upon me there was a resonance in the Scout Scar escarpment whose cliff face habitat is a secret place in the realm of the imagination. The redstarts have chosen a territory close to the popular path and yet out of sight and safe from disturbance. This is a season of redstart for me. I am become confident of their song and I'm seeing a shift in behaviour of the males as they settle into their summer quarters.

Upon Helsington Barrows my favoured larch glade was cool and fragrant, with insects buzzing in sunlight and shadow. Grasshoppers were vocal. All about was purple milkwort and the lemon yellow flowers of mouse-ear hawkweed. The flora of the limestone clitter was beginning to show forth: limestone fern, strawberry and wood sage. Somewhere in the crowns of the deciduous trees a cuckoo called and I glimpsed a bird flying into a solitary oak where he called again. He was mine. If I moved a little closer, never taking my eyes off the oak, I must see him. And he flew veering low to the north and out of sight.

I walked below Scout Scar with long tailed tits flying before me in the tops of the scree-rooted trees. From within the broken down, mossy wall, came the pungent smell of fading ramsons and I could make out the green seed pods of bluebells. Sleek Holstein dairy cattle were recumbent in the pasture and on the path lay a plump lamb that had broken out and come to grief. There are coppiced hazel with staves growing up about them. On the path rising from Barrowfield Farm the guelder rose was coming into bloom, its leaves mined and ruined.

The west-facing limestone cliff; habitat of houry rockrose, Helianthemum canum, *and of* common rockrose, Helianthemum nummularium. 31.3.2008

Monday 4 June 2007: Bradleyfield Allotment and Helsington Barrows

Like the hoary rock rose, mountain everlasting grows on the thin soil close to the escarpment and I found flowers with a delicate pink flush to them. A pipit, beak full of food, still contrived a warning call. I was buzzed by a carrion crow, persistently. A juvenile hopped awkwardly over limestone clitter and I gave it a wide berth, not wide enough for its parents who determined to see me off. A great spotted woodpecker fed in the short grass above Burnbarrow Scar and flew off in alarm when, at last, it saw me.

I was meandering Helsington Barrows when a hare shot away. I looked up high into the crown of an oak to spy out the piping young birds amidst its sun-shot leaves. High on the airy ridges between the dry valleys the view took my breath away: this sweep of landscape from the outliers of the southern Lake District fells to White Cliff, the Kent estuary and toward Barbon and Middleton Fell. The beauty of it sometimes takes me by surprise. Fine tune the senses for the fragrance of Helsington Barrows. Pink larch cones were encrusted with sharp-scented resin sticky on my fingers and a sussuration of breeze in the conifers bore toward me the scent of herbs and Scots pine. The anthills, with their finely worked soil, are the perfect nursery for flora: thyme, milkwort, yellow bird's foot trefoil with its pink claw seed pods and strawberry flowers whose pink runners loop above herbs warmed by the sun and whose leaves conceal fruit on a bed of moss that keeps the plant moist. I picked one warm, sweet strawberry from its herbal bed. Sensational! My thanks to the ants, the fruits of whose labours are delicious. And there was a beautiful clouded buff *Diacrisia sannio*, a moth whose caterpillars feed on heather, violets and plantains.

Wednesday 6 June 2007: Bradleyfield Allotment and Helsington Barrows

Last summer I met Brian Bowness on Bradleyfield and when I mentioned that I'd been out just after 7.00 am he said 'Eh lass, the streets are aired by then'. I determined to do better.

This morning, I awoke to birdsong and was outdoors directly. The Kendal bypass was deserted and silent. The moon showed clear as the sun rose at 4.55 am and curlew called with their lovely bubbling song. On Bradleyfield Allotment larks and pipits were singing and a cuckoo was calling. I spotted a largish bird in characteristic posture: tail raised and wings drooped. My binoculars framed the moon and a cuckoo on the branch of a dead tree. I had the accompaniment of lark song and the rising sun cast a warm glow on the dip slope of the escarpment and my shadow moved before me. Now the cuckoo called from down-slope and throughout my walk there came his intermittent call, sometimes so faint I had to listen intently to pick it up. I love song on the edge of perception: the aural fringe. Listening to bird song one becomes aware of how the acoustic of this place is affected by undulating terrain and exposed rock. Toward the sun, a kestrel hovered. Shortly after sunrise the light was magical with the fells showing the mistiness of the hour. The ridge and the east-facing dip slope were in sunlight whilst Barrowfield Farm and the dark woods around it had yet to receive their wake-up call. They must enjoy the sunset, Bradleyfield the dawn. There was a cool breeze on the escarpment edge and those golden silage fields appeared greenish in a trick of the light. Pipits and stonechats fed their young. The rising sun caught the long stems and flowers of blue moor grass and there was delicate quaking grass and sedges, all caught in the slanting light.

On Helsington Barrows, I came across my first butterfly orchid of the season and dark red helleborine leaves were looking good. It was attractive to stay in the sun so I kept up on the ridge.

Some friends sought a new route last week because of cows newly turned out to pasture and grouped under the trees by the Bradleyfield fields, but I was ready for breakfast so with the slightest shift of line I passed by. This is progress, as my friends will recognise. From the bypass there came the usual drone of fast traffic, that background noise that I suppose I choose not to hear.

During this morning's excursion I met a man walking his dog just before 7.00am and a runner moments later. No-one else. Farmers may well be up and about their work but most of us have lost that natural rhythm of rising with dawn: that day to day contact with the natural world that our ancestors would have taken for granted, which gives an awareness of nature and our interdependence with it. It's the kind of experience so beautifully captured by the nineteenth-century curate Francis Kilvert in his diaries as he walks the Welsh hills visiting his parishioners.

Thursday 7 June 2007: Cunswick Fell and toward Cunswick Tarn

Cunswick Tarn is off limits. But its yellow water lilies and the yellow iris showed forth brightly. Where a track descends into the wood there is a dense patch of gorse and somewhere within it a whitethroat was singing but patience was not rewarded and I could not find it. It was another warm and pleasant day and on the high point of the fell, by the cairn, a lark sang and showed its crest. The ridge had a summer burnished look made up of sorrel, plantains and the flower heads of diverse grasses.

Saturday 9 June 2007: *Bradleyfield Allotment and Helsington Barrows*

On a warm and humid morning, tempted by my tale of sunrise, Monica joined me and we reached Bradleyfield Farm at 4.30 am but this was to be a morning of a different quality. Rosy fingered dawn came not in epic Homeric splendour. Once the sun showed it rose quickly but a dynamic and enveloping mist prevailed, slivers of white clung close to the ground and a heavy dew showed up spiders' webs in the grass. The cuckoo called intermittently, now here, now there, but it flew under cover of the volatile mist which veiled a sun almost as pale as the moon. A wren sang and appeared in profile and without colour. The mist closed in behind us lower down the dip slope, dissolving, shifting, thickening, and the sun was almost blotted out. Toward the escarpment a Welsh Black, reaching up to browse on young ash leaves, loomed out of the mist. Solitary and silent cattle appeared and disappeared. The sun made fitful appearances and the mist disorientated. I thought of Pip out on the Essex marshes and not entirely alone, in that magical opening chapter of *Great Expectations*.

The fells were invisible and Barrowfield Farm was in a pallor of mist with a field half-cut for silage and those familiar vehicles close to the farm ready to complete the task. The hoary rock rose along the cliff edge seemed closed up awaiting the sun and the flowers of *Helianthemum canum* looked more hoar than rose. Natural England is eager to promote the limestone flora and two years ago Richard Gardner of Barrowfield Farm introduced twelve Welsh Black cattle as their manner of grazing is just what is needed. The cows are calving and their

A Welsh Black with backdrop of the fells. This hardy breed grazes throughout the year on the exposed ridge and close to the escarpment edge.

mothers will hide them away in the bracken. The bull is down on the farm and will join them for a few months in August.

On the stile entering the Helsington Barrows enclosure a spider's web drenched in dew trembled in an imperceptible breath of air. There were butterfly orchid and twayblade. The first dropwort of the season showed deep pink buds and its first flowers. Thyme, bedstraw and anthill flora flourished in the hot weather. In the limestone clitter dark red helleborine were in bud. The vista of the Kent estuary was blotted out entirely in the mist that hung low over the anthills.

At about 7.00 am we glimpsed the first dog walker who was swallowed up in the mist, and later several runners. Soon, the sun was breaking through and the light was stronger. Along the escarpment edge I picked up a male redstart with food in his bill. There was a whitethroat in a gorse bush and my wheatear male was out and about with two other birds, so they too have young.

A hot air balloon drifted over the escarpment. In Bristol I used to see and hear them all the time, rarely here.

10 June 2007: *Bradleyfield Allotment and Helsington Barrows*

From 7.00 am. It is the early light I love, and the solitude. It was a warm and sunny morning and Bradleyfield Allotment was rich in birdsong. A curlew flew overhead. The cuckoo was calling and I picked it up in the top of a hawthorn, just within the cluster of fields about Bradleyfield Farm. It flew right over my head to come down in its dead tree perch where first I found it. This open limestone scrub is good cuckoo-locating habitat and Tony Chapman tells me he remembers always finding cuckoo on this very hawthorn from fifty years ago.

Down at Barrowfield Farm silage-making was well underway and amidst several golden fields there remained half a green field and three red tractors at the ready. Contractors come in to make silage, as machinery is so expensive. The grass is cut into two-inch lengths, left for twenty-four hours to wilt, then collected and stored in Richard Gardner's silage barn in a silage clamp. It's a concrete area covered over with plastic sheeting and with tyres on top to seal it as it has to be airtight so that it will ferment. The silage that is fed to the dairy cattle is a yellow/brown colour and smells good to the farmer.

On Helsington Barrows I picked up a male redstart in the top of a larch, pleased to recognise it from a mere snippet of song. A painted lady settled on limestone and it was the season when walking through the seeding grasses raised moths. Yellow lady's bedstraw and St John's wort were coming into flower and I found a cluster of buds, flowers and seed heads of mouse-ear hawkweed. The anthill flora was a delight. There were two wrecked anthills, their mounds sliced off, but this time the culprit had left DNA at the scene in the form of dried out pats of dung. A Galloway did it. Strawberries love the limestone clitter and throw out runners across the rock, then flower and fruit. Yesterday male linnet eluded us, but today he showed. As I walked across the Barrows, with the Kent estuary in view, a piping sound came from a Scots pine and it proved to be a family of coal tit feeding.

By 10.00am it was hot and two boys on mountain bikes took the rocky path along the Scar. Below the trig point, three runners hailed me and scared small birds out of the trees. Green sloes and juniper berries were forming and wild roses had a delicate fragrance.

16 June 2007: *Bradleyfield Farm and Scout Scar*

I walked up to Bradleyfield Farm to see the swallows in the byres and the yard was full of bleating sheep and lambs which were being sprayed. April was hot and dry which stimulated blowfly pupae in the soil to hatch and toward the end of the month they found early evidence, hence the spraying. Flies are attracted to lay their eggs in bad feet, then the sheep lies down with its feet beneath its body and wicks or maggots grow into the flesh. Flies exploit a scratch, a wound, or a mucky spot and lay eggs and that vulnerable strike area attracts more blowflies. Eggs hatch rapidly in sunny weather and maggots can appear on a dead sheep within a few days. Clipping is a preventive measure against blowfly strike and sheep are less likely to be stranded on their backs if they have been clipped. I had arrived at a busy time but Brian Bowness paused to explain what they were doing and why.

He had hoped to be clipping but throughout last week the weather had been cold, wet and windy and so that had to be postponed. Some of the lambs born in late April were struggling with pneumonia and were injected to help them through. He has almost 300 sheep which he now grazes on the race course and on the in-bye land. 116 hogs (last year's lambs) will go into his breeding stock at Potter Fell. One or two might be struggling but many of them look plump and robust. In a byre are large hessian wool bags with fleeces off the one year old hogs, ready to be sent off to the Wool Marketing Board. They are folded, white side out, according to the variety of sheep. These are cold fleeces but when warm they are running wet with lanolin which is sticky and softens the hands of the clipper. Nowadays, only the whole fleece can be sold so they try to remove it in a single piece. They start with the belly and that wool is thrown away. The scraps, or lock-ins, used to be bagged and sold too. Now they are worthless. Economically, the wool fetches little and sheep are farmed for meat. They are sold as lamb when they still have their lamb's teeth and before they are a year old.

Out on the eaves and roof-ridges some of the swallows had fledglings being fed and learning to fly. Others swooped into the byre and made for their nests high in the intersections of the whitewashed wall and purlins. There was the sound of wings sweeping through the gloom and adults called to their cheeping nestlings who awaited the next feed. The floor was spattered with bird shit. From beyond the byre came the call of a curlew, of chickens and the loud bleating of sheep in the farm yard. The farmer likes to see swallows in his barns and so doors are left open to welcome them.

Out on Bradleyfield Allotment the sun shone and there was an intensity of colour in the landscape that often comes after rain. The Howgills were in deep indigo, there was blue sky overhead and brilliant white Cumulus cloud below it. Grasshopper were chirruping and I came across a couple and their young son engrossed in catching them. The boy had caught some twenty and he showed me how he went about it. His father told me it needed a quick eye.

Returning down Brigsteer Road we met again and the conversation turned to wildlife finds in the locality; this summer and in recent years. This is an invaluable way of learning and it's also a kind of community bonding. It declares who looks, who sees, who cares and who is keeping a record. This couple captured the 2004 waxwing flock on video as the birds fed in their garden in Cedar Grove. And it was good to see a boy so captivated by wildlife.

Twice this summer, whilst out walking, I have fallen into conversation with someone who has shown me mobile phone clips of peregrines: one nesting at St Bees Head, another feeding on its kill in the heart of Kendal at the Brewery Arts Centre! The mobile and the digital camera offer a currency for birding, a validation. I've heard tales apocryphal of a golden age of birding: an afternoon when eight cuckoos were sighted on Helsington Barrows! Perhaps some twenty five years ago it was possible to meet with such an abundance of cuckoos. How may we know whom we might credit, whose authority is to be relied on? Speculating on the question of verification Gilbert White tells his reader *a sober hind* assured him. Well I meet several such sober hinds about Scout Scar.

Sunday 17 June 2007: *Bradleyfield Allotment and Helsington Barrows*

The day was warm and humid with flies pestering and after reading up on blow fly strike yesterday I felt itchy.

There were drifts of white flowers on Helsington Barrows: lavish dropwort, bedstraw and butterfly orchid. There was lady's bedstraw and the first harebell and fragrant orchid and there was an exquisite fragrance abroad.

It's a time of year that calls for particular attention when birdwatching. There were juveniles galore and sometimes a bush revealed a surprising variety of species.

Skylark and pipit were singing and soaring and there were families of wheatear and stonechat. Parent birds were on the *qui vive* and I heard a female redstart, with a beak stuffed with food, calling to alert its young to keep quiet and it stayed perched until I moved on.

20 June 2007: *Bradleyfield Allotment and Scout Scar*

The season of lark song is enchanting. I love finding that speck in the clouds, watching the bird close its wings, its song cutting out somewhere on that plummet to earth. There was a strong wind which played through the seeding flowers of the tall grasses.

On the ridge, there is a high-line with a panorama of almost 360 degrees. And Kendal was invisible below.

There was St John's wort and early scabious. Everywhere white bedstraw and yellow lady's bedstraw. And harebell which can be found as late as October.

I met Tony Chapman who knows of the peregrine of Kendal quarry and he drove me out there to see if we could locate it. There were jackdaw and black headed gulls but no raptors. Next day, I had tea with Irene who remembers going onto the golf course with her husband and a telescope to seek out the nesting peregrine some fifteen years ago.

26 June 2007: *Bradleyfield Allotment and Helsington Barrows*

June has been very wet and yesterday there was 100mm of rain in twenty-four hours and Sheffield recorded its highest rainfall ever. A consequence of climate change? David Miliband, environment secretary on this the last day of Blair's premiership, cautiously stated that this was an extreme weather event (a feature of climate change) and there are more of them. South Cumbria was on the edge of this swathe of high winds, including several recorded tornadoes, and torrential rain. But it was too rough to tempt me out. Wildlife makes itself scarce in such weather.

Today there was clarity and an intensity of colour that often comes in the aftermath of a storm. The Langdale Pikes showed forth in sunshine and shadow. To the south, the tide was far out and the Kent estuary and Morecambe Bay showed rosy sands with a deep blue line of the sea beyond. Excellent visibility and depth of colour. The sunlight depicted features on Arnside and Silverdale Moss as I had never seen them, and distant Heysham Power Station loomed large and the sweep of coast and Blackpool Tower showed clearly: Blackpool illuminations.

Summer branches have been ripped from the beeches of Beast Banks. Quite how much havoc was wreaked amidst the wildlife on the exposed scrub of

Bradleyfield Allotment and Helsington Barrows it is impossible to know. My wheatear family looked as if their feathers had been ruffled and two of them were heads down and preening. An adult kestrel sat in the sun beside its nest niche. Another hung in the wind, hunting over the escarpment edge. Bracken spurted into growth and it was apparent just how much there is, plenty for Welsh Blacks careful of their calves. Wood sage was flowering, with attractive pale flower heads. The flora on the ridge was lovely: drifts and clusters of dropwort, white clover, yellow lady's mantle. Dark red helleborine is more widely dispersed over the Barrows than I had realised and I found several new sites. A pipit came parachuting down on rigid wings and landed with a trill in a hawthorn. Toward the race course, I found some fifty fragrant orchid in a dense cluster.

7 July 2007: Low Plantation, Barrowfield Lot and Honeybee Wood

Yet more rain but the day improved, and when six of us on a Kendal Naturalists meet reached a clear-felled area where hardwoods had been planted there was a butterfly diversion, with dark green fritillaries and meadow browns feeding on brambles. There was red bartsia along the path-side and ragwort smothered in the black and yellow striped caterpillars of the cinnabar moth (*Tyria jacobaeae*), some so tiny they seemed almost black. There were drifts of wavy hair grass, delicate with golden seed heads and red stems. Siskin flew over Barrowfield Farm. As we came out of the wood a southern hawker was caught in the sunlight.

14 July 2007: Bradleyfield Allotment and Helsington Barrows

Some generations are unlucky with the year of their birth. For some species this must be a disastrous summer. Yesterday and this morning there was rain, and rain with thunder is forecast for tomorrow. The day gradually improved and late afternoon was rather fine with blue sky, Cumulus and a stiff breeze. There were a few fritillaries about and I saw a solitary blue. At this season the path-side flowers beyond Bradleyfield come into their own: scabious, harebell, sweet smelling lady's bedstraw and fresh frog orchid with a purplish brown tinge to them. Close by are drifts of waving reddish-gold grasses. The dark red helleborine are at their best. Thyme and squinancywort grow along the path which follows the escarpment edge. Squinancywort is a tiny woodruff with a hint of pink, unheeded even as people walk upon it. A walker asked me if I had seen a deer in a pasture close to Barrowfield Farm below. I had not. I was eyes down and enjoying the flowers. No-one sees it all and that's the hook: there's always more to discover.

The Bradleyfield ewes had been clipped and sculpted lines showed on their bodies. They looked haggard compared to the cream-fleeced and plump lambs that frisked about.

Sunday 15 July 2007: *Bradleyfield Allotment and Scout Scar*

A still, humid and warm day with thunderstorms scheduled to reach us mid-afternoon. On the doorstep I looked up from lacing my boots to see a peregrine soaring on an updraught, against blue sky and white Cumulus.

The sky was full of swifts. At the ghyll, a moustached wren, her beak stuffed with a long-legged fly, was busy about the mossy wall. She flitted about warily making no attempt to eat her insect which was probably for her brood. A buzzard sat close to the kestrel nest and the only kestrel I saw was a bird hunting on Bradleyfield Allotment.

In the stillness and warmth a fragrance rose from the path-side flora: lady's bedstraw, scabious, dropwort, clovers. There are stonechat about and I hear linnet. The male wheatear is sentinel on his stones.

18 July 2007: *Farm walk at Cinderbarrow, Levens*

Situated on the limestone just above the Levens mosses, Cinderbarrow is a National Trust farm, formerly part of the Sizergh estate. There was a warm welcome from farmers David and Rose Willison as folk gathered early on a fine evening with swallows flitting about the farm. Their new Jersey dairy herd was a change for them and they awaited the installation of a new milking parlour, appropriate for this smaller breed. There is auto ID for each cow, whose milk is chilled down to 3 degrees and collected every other day. From this coming October it would be used for luxury Jersey yogurts. What a pity Brussels regulations allowed Rose to offer us a cup of tea but not a glass of milk from their Jerseys. Such is bureaucracy. As we crossed the yard David explained that you judge the health of a cow by the condition of its dung and he looks for fibre. The evidence lay at our feet. Prolonged periods of rain can produce 'water grass', with a very high water content. Dry matter is an essential part of the cows' diet and they are free to wander indoors to feed on silage which has been mixed with meal, wheat, soya and some straw. A nutritionist advises on their feed and a computerised diet feeder monitors the average consumption of feed per cow. When they are indoors during the winter the farmer knows exactly how much each cow is getting. The Jersey bull is not let out because 'he's mean' – it's in the genes. Rose has looked after calves for the last 30 years and these three week old Jerseys were delightful. They nuzzled against her and sucked her fingers as she stroked their throats which they lifted up to her. They've clearly bonded with her but they are confiding creatures and we all fell for them. I found my shirt being gently chewed and my knees being licked by warm, wet tongues. Sensational! She showed us the new computerised feeding station. A calf enters and the machine reads a transponder on a collar about its neck and mixes its personal feed of powdered milk; it has eight a day. There is also cow cake in a trough right by the milk supply so the calves get used to taking both.

David Willison showed us samples of his wool clip: a cream-coloured fleece which he can sell, a Swaledale fleece with a streak of black wool that renders it almost worthless and an all black fleece which is without value. He has to pay for this unsaleable wool to be taken off the farm because regulations prevent his burning it. Only green waste, like hedge trimmings, may be burnt on site. He clips his own sheep because to contract it out would cost £1000 for his 1000 sheep and a fleece sells for £1 – exactly the price it fetched 55 years ago when his father began farming. Kendal 's motto boasts *pannus mihi panis*, 'wool is my bread': an anachronism since David Willison keeps sheep for the sale of lambs and wool is merely a by-product. Fleeces, off cuts and dag wool used to be washed in the River Kent. These days the health of river systems is high on the environmental agenda and cleaning dirty wool is costly in consequence.

Cinderbarrow Farm is situated where the limestone escarpment runs down to meet the mosses and looks out across the Lyth Valley. David Willison pointed out a pond which receives run-off, a safety barrier between farmyard and catchwater. Brian Fereday advised on the reed bed which filters it most effectively before cleaned water joins the catchwater to flow south into the River Kent. Yesterday's downpours must have tested it and he told of a deluge sweeping down the yard. We crossed over the catchwater and looked north at a cluster of field strips and a copse on the vestigial peat of Park Moss, below Brigsteer Park. The old houses of Cotes and Brigsteer have rights of common of turbary; peat may be cut from a specific piece of land if there is any left. Cotes itself marks the place where peat cutters lived and they stored the peat they dug out in cotes, meaning stores or shelters. Our walk took us onto the Levens mosses, with fields defined by hedge, ditch and drain. David Willison explained the regime of hedge laying Cumberland style: stems and branches are removed and only the main stems (liggers) are laid low to the ground. When they took over the farm in 1998 the hedges had not been attended to for years and had grown old, grown out, and sheep could get through. Hedges are important both for stock control and ecologically and little birds thrive in the hedgerow we followed on our return walk along Fiddlers' Causeway. A swan had six cygnets here last summer and, further along the catchwater, had raised three this year. He is not the first farmer to mention how wildlife thrived during the Foot and Mouth epidemic of 2001 when access was prohibited.

The news is dominated by floods in the UK and this summer matures into the wettest since records began. Farm walks prove the perfect opportunity to fetch out my high Arctic green wellingtons, just high enough to keep my knees dry against the 'wetting up' field where we sloshed through long grass deep in water. It's a field designed for waders of one sort or another. A system of drain, ditch, sluice and bund typical of the Lyth Valley is here directed to keeping the water table high so that the area will 'go back to nature', a quiet, unvisited wetland ideal to attract breeding yellow wagtail, redshank, curlew and lapwing. High water levels in ditches provide shallow pools for feeding birds and David Willison keeps a few cattle here so that their trampling creates a habitat of rush tussocks and waterlogged pockets. 'Wetting up' is part of a Cumbria-specific project, targeted at improved pasture which was formerly wet grassland, with the aim of reversing the decline in numbers of redshank and yellow wagtail. Cinderbarrow Farm lies within one of the target areas: the Kent estuary and the Morecambe Bay Limestones. The RSPB monitor the zone six times a year and are hopeful of the success of these returned-to-wetland areas within the Lyth Valley. This project was initiated in 2003 and when DEFRA came to monitor during the flood of January 2005 there was water up to the hedge tops; obvious wetland potential.

The success of dairy farming in the Lyth Valley is reliant upon the pumping system. Rose and David Willison have 70 acres in use for silage to make winter fodder for their Jerseys which like a long cut of grass. So they take two good cuts a season. If the mosses were flooded deeper and for longer, as they would be without the pumps, then the Willisons would have to cut silage later and would probably get only one cut.

Farmers are working hard to manage the environment and produce food and now there comes a third element in the equation: bio energy. Some wheat is grown on Cinderbarrow Farm and in the Lyth Valley and fetches high prices if grown as a first generation bio fuel crop. Environmental organisations are watching this development closely, to see what impact this change will have, and the RSPB has just put out a report on bio energy in the UK.

The introduction of Galloway cattle to the National Trust area of Helsington Barrows was controversial because there had not been cattle on that land for over 100 years. The National Trust and Natural England (English Nature until 2006) wanted a different grazing regime to encourage flora and this was under discussion in 2001 at the time of the Foot and Mouth outbreak. For the farmers, the welfare of their cattle would determine the choice of breed which would be out on the Barrows all year round and would need to be hardy. There are yew trees and there was a concern yew would prove toxic if eaten. In his *Antiquities of Selborne Letter V*, Gilbert White wrote that a female yew tree shed its berries in the street and he noted the results when hogs, horses and cows ate twigs, leaves or berries. It is a debate of long standing.

Bracken can also be toxic and ticks can result in tick fever which causes cattle to abort. The seventeen Galloways came from the mountains of Mull and were accustomed to bracken and ticks and Rose was told they would resist everything except a bullet!

The Willisons have a new bull this season and he was up there now for six weeks. He was checked before being turned out but with cows there they tend to be fine. The cows finished calving toward the end of May and into June when there is most grass, so they will give plenty of milk. The heiffers are pedigree and perhaps breed only every other year but that is not a concern because the cattle are primarily a management tool. Ultimately, they provide beef and very good it is too. Grazing on the fragrant herbs of Helsington Barrows it should be something special. They must be slaughtered before 30 months but the Willisons like to keep them as close as possible to that date so the beef is mature. There is no standing water on the limestone of Helsington Barrows so there is a water trough with a header tank that usually fills itself. Last summer a bowser was needed up there. They check the Galloways every other day and the cows come running at the beep of a horn, to be rewarded with a bit of cow cake each. This is to keep them humanised because they go through the usual regime of being tagged and TB tested and the Willisons would not want them to go feral. The only time these cows are edgy is in the three to four days after a calf is born. The hound trailing fraternity train up there and a puppy found a calf in the bracken which bawled for its mother who came running and next moment the young hound hurtled through the air. The Galloways are a great success. The yew presents them with no problem and they graze all over the area, which is just what was intended. I can verify that from the distribution of cow pats and the bulldozed anthills.

We drove home to Kendal along the Brigsteer Road to a fine sunset and images of a barn owl which rose on languid wings and dipped out of sight to reappear again and again in ghostly pallor about the deep summer foliage of a hedgerow.

During the farm walk David Willison was speaking of the 2001 Foot and Mouth outbreak. 'It will come back', he said, 'it will come back'. He could not have envisaged the virus would escape from the government laboratories at Purbright, courtesy of Merial, and since it showed on 3rd August the leak must have been happening as he spoke.

I met Rose Willison on 14 January 2008, on a National Trust walk on the Lyth Valley mosses led by Brian Fereday. The Willisons had received their wool cheque and prices averaged out at 27 pence a fleece! At Bradleyfield, Brian Bowness had the same experience.

24 July 2007: *Bradleyfield Allotment to Cunswick Fell*

At noon yesterday there was a dramatic thunderstorm over Kendal but this was nothing compared to the floods and the desperate plight of towns and cities along the course of the Severn and Thames. The jet stream seemed locked over England and this would prove to be the wettest July, the wettest English summer, on record.

Today there was respite from the downpours. Beyond the race course, there was lady's bedstraw with diverse harebells, scabious and a goodly scattering of frog orchid in the short turf.

There had been a few ominous clouds but as we reach Cunswick Fell the day became warmer and the line of fells showed up clear. There is a mass of gorse just where a footpath descends to Cunswick Tarn and amidst the short turf I spied autumn gentian, its flowers wide open in response to the sun. I heard linnet overhead and soon came upon a bird in the top of a hawthorn but we were looking directly into the sun and all we saw was a small bill and a silhouette, so we tentatively made our way around it in the hope of a better view. All this while we were on tenterhooks (a local affliction as we were not far from historic sites of tenter fields where woollen cloth was stretched on frames after being cleaned in a fulling mill). Excitement mounted; my linnet sightings had been few this year. And there it was: the perfectly posed, perfectly lit male linnet with rosy head and breast.

Back home, I listened to my new voice recorder which captured our in-the-field suspense and its resolution, the breathy excitement of a discovery.

30 July 2007: *Bradleyfield Allotment and Helsington Barrows*

Heather was coming into bloom and this is its season of splendour. Above Burnbarrow Scar sloes were ripening on the stunted plants about the limestone clitter. A family of coal tits showed in a larch and a buzzard perched in a dead tree. Heading for home, I saw a flash of an orange tail and watched a male redstart in hawthorn for some while.

31 July 2007: *Scout Scar and Helsington Barrows*

Fine altocumulus began the morning. A kestrel hovered against the blue and a pair of ravens soared. Held on a thermal was a trio of paragliders over Helsington Barrows.

Soundscape of grasshoppers, and noisy woodwork which resolved itself as a great spotted woodpecker climbing a larch and a nuthatch in an oak tree. It was the summer holidays and the drone of speed boats was audible from Windermere.

A reprise of my Breughel scene as farmers made good use of a couple of fine days to cut and bring in the silage. Barrowfield was cutting yesterday, today Tullythwaite Hall has its shuttle of colourful tractors, silage harvester and container truck. From high up on Scout Scar the patterns down below in the Lyth Valley were mesmerising: straight lines and curves about the corners of fields, about an excrescence of limestone. On the fringe of this summer's dreadful weather, the farmers may bring in enough winter fodder for their cattle if they are fortunate.

Here were more dark red helleborine just as the light was perfect. There is a toppled dead tree and on the highest tip of its antler-like branches sat a spotted flycatcher. Now in an oak, whose crown is spiked with small, dead branches, the bird flew up and came down each time on a bare branch. There was an abundance of flies today, noisy and pestering. Rather less as the flycatcher picked them off. In a butterfly-like move it flitted about and perched with another of its kind.

I was walking right on the edge above Scout Scar escarpment and there at my feet was the exquisite squinancywort against a foil of rock. When I knelt to look I saw a single flower of autumn gentian amidst thyme and the delicate pink squinancywort. A fine mosaic of flowers.

7 August 2007: Scout Scar

Yesterday the Barrowfield Welsh Blacks were right on the escarpment edge; cows with several calves and a neat bull.

22 August 2007: Bradleyfield Allotment and Helsington Barrows

Met Brian Bowness and Tony Chapman on the race course a couple of days ago and had an update on the swallows of Bradleyfield Farm which could not feed, probably because of the relentless rain and cold. Naked nestlings fell out of the nest dead. The farm's position affords a degree of shelter but it is on the 140 meter contour. At any rate their swallows are gone. Gilbert White puzzled over how hirundines survived appalling late spring weather. Just what is happening when they're out of sight? Trying to make sense of the wildlife scene during these extreme weather events is difficult.

The heather was deep in colour and fragrant and the grasshoppers were vocal on a fine summer's day with a breeze. This was the time for felwort, dark-coloured leaves and spikes of the plants showed beside the path just beyond the race course.

Every flower I have found hereabouts can be seen without leaving a path, except

A mosaic of flowers on the limestone of the escarpment edge. Top left: a single flower of felwort, Gentianella amarella. *Left: spilling over the rock is squinancywort,* Asperula cynanchica. *The darker purple flowers are thyme and its leaves show against the rock.*

rue leaved saxifrage. About Helsington Barrows there were both white and purple felwort flowers and I stopped to chat with a woman with whom I swop finds when we chance to meet up here. She had seen spotted fly catcher at Bradleyfield Farm, close to my location of last summer. Every time I headed up that way I had checked it out, with no luck. Homeward bound, I gave my tree a glance before reaching the spot she had described. There they were on the dead branches of shrubs of the in-bye land, just where they had been last summer, two playful birds. She must have called them up. Excellent views, I have an indifferent photograph. I had heard that flycatcher, being a late-arriving migrant, had hit the foul weather and fared badly this summer but I found both my last summer's families in situ. With the erratic weather we are having however do migrants gauge things? If the spotted flycatcher arrived expecting a repeat of last summer they were in for a shock.

On bonfire night I was reading Thomas Bewick's *A History of British Birds* and his description of spotted flycatcher feeding struck a chord. It is strangely moving to find he saw a moment of flight, 'like that of a butterfly'. It felt like a hotline to a late eighteenth century naturalist.

3 and 9 September 2007: *a valedictory. Swallows and damsons in the Lyth Valley*

A few swallows skimmed the Scout Scar escarpment where the scent of heather was strong, its flowers soon to fade. A flock of linnets flew by and above Burnbarrow Scar, by the gate onto Helsington Barrows; I heard hammerings and tappings in the larch and found tree creeper, a flock of long tailed tits, coal tits and a great spotted woodpecker. There was a remarkable defining light and shadow on the fells so I walked back along the escarpment edge and could make out the clefts coming down from Dow Crag and the track up to Coniston Old Man.

In the early afternoon I drove across the Lyth Valley by Toll Bar Cottage, busy with house martins and where rose bay willowherb, resplendent in the strong sun, was losing its damask flowers to the curlicues of exploded seed capsules. Low Farm, my destination, is below The Howe at no more than 14 metres, on the spring line where the limestone meets the peat mosses. Anne Wilson has a well in her main yard. Her farmhouse lies just above the River Gilpin where she has seen otter whilst walking her dog. It was the time of the damson harvest. Between customers, Andy rinsed the luscious fruit and filled a demi-john to which he would add sugar and gin. Damsons bought on the morning of their picking when the bloom was still on them. Despite months of rain there was a fine crop, unlike last year. Damsons thrive here on the limestone, on lichen-encrusted trees that are pruned and can live to 30 years old. The farms hereabouts have contracts for the sale of their damsons and sell direct from the farm too. Anne has recently converted some old farm buildings into work units and lets them for the making of furniture and wooden lodges. Tradition side by side with change as farmers are forced to diversify. They have kept two of the old barns and offer hospitality to swallows who have raised two broods. We talked birds and Andy showed me a clip

Damson trees in a hedgerow above Low Farm looking east across the upper reaches of the Lyth Valley toward the Scout Scar escarpment. 12.4.2008

he had captured on his mobile phone of a peregrine which had just made a kill at the Brewery Arts Centre in Kendal! Rooks and crows were taking their ripe pears. Farmers know who hosts what in the Lyth Valley and I heard of a barn owl and a tawny owl. I assume these cherished birds are ex-directory, confided within a trusted fellowship. Certainly some farmers prefer that locations are not disclosed.

Just up the road at Dawson Fold there is a roadside fruit and vegetable stall and one September the lady who runs it had placed over-ripe fruit on a low wall to distract wasps from her produce and had created a side-show of fruit smothered in Whitbarrow butterflies. Today, a garden clothesline was jaunty with colourful plastic pegs and a high wire above her stall was strung with swallows. 'My twittering friends. One day soon it will be silent and they will be gone.' They are her summer guests and nest in her barns, her companions through the season. On the wire were glossy-backed adults with long streamers and pointed wings, their legs tucked in beneath them in a classic posture. But on a hot afternoon at Low Farm there was something else. Families of swallows relaxed on the warm slates of the barn roof, splayed out, displayed so their soft and intimate plumage was opened up to the sun, exposed. Abandon on a barn roof. It's rare to see their white-feathered thighs; it was a revelation. A passing car spooked them and they swirled into the air but soon settled again and resumed their preening, their long wings extended and angled out. Many were young birds whose plumage was soft greys and whites, their throats creamy, the long, adult streamers yet to come. They sunbathed, rid themselves of parasites, sleeked up their feathers, checked them over in readiness for the long-haul flight to Africa. They were feeding up for that amazing journey. Soon, so soon they would be gone, these sociable and beloved birds.

At Selborne on 13 September 1791 Gilbert White studied this same behaviour in gathering swallows and he too was enchanted by it. And puzzled. What did their disappearance signify? Did they 'emigrate' or hibernate? Then and now migration holds elements of mystery and awe. Within that sociable twittering what might they communicate about the practicalities of their long journey: destination, navigation, when to go?

Andy would like to ring his Low Farm swallows to celebrate their safe return next spring, this kinship group. A ring in token of the bond forged between them: the swallows who are his welcome visitors. Wedded to the swallows with their seasonal migration: their coming with the promise of spring as daylight hours grow longer and temperatures rise, their departure in early autumn as days grow shorter and temperatures fall.

The damson harvest gained momentum as they prepared to leave. They would be missed, the swallows. But soon fieldfare and redwing would arrive from the north to take advantage of the season's berries, on passage and to overwinter.